Religious Revitalisation Movements in Manipur

RELIGIOUS REVITALISATION MOVEMENTS IN MANIPUR

Naorem Joykumar Singh

AKANSHA PUBLISHING HOUSE
NEW DELHI • GUWAHATI • VISAKHAPATNAM

AKANSHA PUBLISHING HOUSE
4649-B/21, Ansari Road
Darya Ganj, New Delhi - 110 002
Ph.: 23263193 / 9811582579 / 09435116718
Fax: 011-23263193
Email: ektabooks@yahoo.com
www.akanshapublishinghouse.com

Religious Revitalisation Movements in Manipur

First Published 2012
ISBN 978-81-8370-304-8

PRINTED IN INDIA

Published by Akansha Publishing House, New Delhi and Printed at Harmain Offset, Delhi.

Dedicated

To

Naoria Phullo

Who laid the foundation for the growth of the idea of self determination among the Manipuris

Contents

Foreword

The two most important divine personalities in the pantheon are Sanamahi and Pakhangba. Of the two, more popular is Sanamahi who had later developed into a cult popularly known as Sanamahi cult. The greatness of Sanamahi lies in the fact that he is the creator of the world and mankind. So the south-west corner of every Meitei home is reserved for Sanamahi or Snamhi Kachin which is believed to be the abode of *Lai*.

It is generally believed that Khagemba was the first Meitei king who popularized the worship of Sanamahi. Ironically, Khagemba's reign also witnessed the beginning of the Brahmanical influence in Manipur. But it was Maharaja Garibniwaz who actually got converted into a Hindu and then imposed Hinduism as a state religion in Manipur since 1724 A.D. As a result, the indigenous Meitei religion was being colored by many Hindu codes and rites. However, unhappy with the king and his new religion was a man called Lourembam Khongnangthaba who left Manipur and waited for the revival of the original Meitei religion centering around the worship of Sanamahi. It is stated that Lourembam Khongnangthaba, disguised as Sadhu, appeared before Naoria Phullo, born and brought up in Cachar 200 years after his departure from Manipur and then entrusted the task of reviving the original Meitei religion to him (Phullo). It is also stated Khongnangthaba gave a small box to Phullo containing scriptures on Meitei religion and culture.

In this way, Naoria Phullo thus set to revive and revitalize the philosophy and concept of the primal religion of the Meiteis by establishing the Apokpa Marup at Laishram Khul, Jafribon, Cachar in 1930. Another organization called Meitei Marup was also established by Takhellambam Bokul, one of the most prominent followers of Phullo.

Right from the beginning, the revival movement met with serious and opposition from the Hinduised Meiteis who had the support of the Meitei king. By the 70s of the 20th century, the revival movement slowly gained strong foundation and became popular particularly among the educated youths of the state. At times the movement assumed revolutionary character and this conflict between the Meitei revivalists and the pro-Hindu Meiteis has still been an unending process in present Meitei society.

Prof N. Joykumar, who has a strong scholastic foundation in the history of North East India, particularly the history of Manipur, has taken this sensitive issue in right earnest. His command over the sources, the methodology he has adopted in studying the problem and his analysis on the multi-dimensional aspects of the revival movement is really illuminating. In the book Prof. Joykumar has revealed much new information hitherto unearthed which are in fact his unique contributions towards the enrichment of our knowledge on the subject.

Prof. Lal Dena

Manipur University

Preface

The growth of conflict over the ideology and nature of practice between the Hinduism and primal religion which some people used to call it 'Sanamahism' is a new phenomenon in the ongoing courses of the History of Manipur. The tendency for the growth of this religious conflict was started from the first part of the twentieth century. It is a well aware fact that the religious idea and practices of Hinduism had entered into Manipur during the last part of seventeenth century and it was fully flourished during the eighteenth century. Since then the ideology and practices Hinduism began to move her journey as a state religion. Apart from this it also produced a serious impact in the social, cultural, even to the economic life of the people of Manipur particularly in the valley areas. The establishment of Brahma Sabha, a religious organisation of Hinduism and its nature of working style had also brought some kind of unhappiness and undesirable changes in the mindset of the people. The introduction of clean and unclean system in the society was one of the biggest problems faced by the people. And many people became the victim of this policy of ostracism. So this social ostracism policy had further intensified the anger of the people to the nature of the Brahma Sabha. But due to the presence of strong patronage of the king the people were not able to express their unhappiness openly. Therefore for quite long time the people, with great patience were waiting for an opportune time to express their anger against the social ostracism policy of the Brahma Sabha. Finally the people were able to get this long awaited opportunity only when one Naoria Phullo had started to express openly against the policy of Brahmins. After this a new idea had developed to revitalize the primary religion of this country and in course of time the anti-Brahman elements in the society had started to formule an idea for the materialisation of their objective and started to translate it in the form of a mass movement.

Since then the people had witnessed the different phases of the nature of participation of the people in the process of religious revitalization movement. There are so many informations about the nature of the activities of the movement. But still we are not able to give a scientific analysis about the character of the movement from a certain theoretical framework. The main objective of this work is to make an attempt to give a complete picture about the nature of the movement including the different stages of the growth of anti-Hinduism stand within the framework of a conceptual theory. In this venture I was able to get support from many quarters. Particularly I would like to mention the name of Prof. Lal Dena for his priceless support and contribution during the period of the preparation of my monograph. Without his sincere help, I am afraid, I may not be able to translate all my efforts to realities. I also thank all the faculty members of History Department including my students for their moral support. I also would like to extend my heartiest thank to my beloved brother Shri Oinam Krishna Singh who always takes a great pain in typing my monograph. I also thank all the employees in the Department particularly N. Lalitkumar Singh, Baleswor Singh and Joy Kabui for their valuable physical help for the success of my effort. I also thank all the members of my family including my sons and daughters for their positive role in the process of the completion of my work. Finally I thank Mr. M.P. Misra, Akansha Publishing House, New Delhi, for changing my monograph in the form of book. To me he is a great friend who always supports my academic ventures.

N. Joykumar Singh

1

Introduction

The disintegration and reorganisation are an integral part of the society. This is the outcome of ideological conflict between the old guard and radical section of the society who strongly advocated for the maintenance of their respective social and cultural perspective. The conflict between these two ideologies had always been manifested in different characters. At the same time such type of dialectical approach is also a great contributory factor to the growth of society towards a more positive direction. Within the natural framework of these norms the people had also actively participated in the process of development of their society right from the time immemorial. There is no limit to the growth of human knowledge. So, as the people had earned more knowledge and advancement in every aspect of the social life they always tried to look forward to a more meaningful and positive development. The impact of this fast changing phenomenon had produced an ideological gap between old social expectation and new social behavior. So the demand for a new social behavior is always manifested in the form of a movement. Forced deculturation, social segregation, simple cultural diversity, social cultural disorganization, economic and social exploitation, political and social domination etc. are some specific areas where the radical section of the society had strongly advocated for a change so that a new social order could be established very effectively. It is also mentioned that these movements for change are 'exogenous'and 'acculturative'[1] because they arose from the contact of the traditional cultural values with that of modern material outlook. Vittorio Lanternari regarded such type of movement as 'highly impressive manifestation of the acculturative process'.[2] It is a well aware fact that a movement is a series of action and endeavours' by a body of persons for a special objective. The body of persons means the members of the society who believed in the new social behaviour. The sole objective of the movement is to give a new direction in the social, cultural, political and religious life of the society. Such type of dialectical approach always brought forth new positive changes with fresh idea and principles in every aspects of social life. In later years the behavioral scientists have classified these movements on the basis of their salient characteristics, nature of activities and ideologies in different conceptual frameworks like 'Nativistic Movement', 'Reform Movement', 'Millenarian Movement', 'Messianic Movement', 'Revolutionary Movement', Charismatic Movement', etc. The people always make an attempt to bring about a new order only when traditional institutions are unable to adapt and response to the changing pattern in the social life. Loren Von Stein, who was regarded as one of the pioneers in the study of the social movements, made a clear observation about the character of the human beings. He said, "since life represents a constant struggle of the personnel self-determining element with non-personnel element, the life of human community is a permanent struggle between state and society".[3] On the other hand the people who refused to accept the changes always tried to resist the new trend. As a result of this, a reactionary idea came out from the unhappy marginal people and challenged the existing status quo in the character of the society. So when a collective attempt was made to bring about a change in the existing system or to create an entirely new order such mass involvement phenomenon is regarded as a movement.

A.F.C.Wallace, a renowned social anthropologist, was of the view that the concept and character of various types of movement are of the same uniform process. Their only ultimate object was to bring about a new innovation in the existing social order. So since the collective efforts of the masses aimed for a radical change and having a uniform process in the nature and character he proposed to use a term called 'Revitalisation Movement'. The literal meaning of the term 'revitalise' means to give a new life or imbue with the new life and vitality. It is said that he developed this idea after having the experience of a biographical research of the new religion of one Handsome Lake which was introduced to the Iroquois in the early 1800 A.D. According to Wallace revitalisation movement is "a deliberate, organized conscious effort by members of a society to construct a more satisfying culture".[4] His idea for the construction of a more satisfying culture has clearly manifested as a character of the changing phenomenon of the people when the existing social order is not satisfactory to them. To look forward for a more radical change is the real nature of the developmental process. The social conflict and its alienation and antagonism is the natural phenomena of the existing society. Wallace also strongly emphasized the immediate need for a mass involvement for going towards a successful attempt in the process of the establishment of a new culture. The action of the mass involvement or social collectivism is a spontaneous work for those people who strongly advocated for a radical change in the social order and cultural life. In addition to this he also stressed the importance of the leader or prophet who was supposed to take the responsibilities of stewardship of the movement. He further said that the outbreak of such type of new phenomenon and its activities are always centered around through the code and sacred message of a charismatic leader who called for a radical change.[5] According to him, the persons involved in the process of revitalization should have the capabilities to perceive the existing system or norms either in culture or religion and they must feel that this system is unsatisfactory. Apart from this he also suggested that the person who involves in the process should not confine only to the innovation of discrete items but they should also try to see new order and system in the life of the given society. But change in the existing social and cultural order cannot be materialised on the deliberate intention of the interested members of the society. It is made possible only when the people fully understand the chain reaction and resultant effect which was in process from one generation to another. The endless chain reaction automatically shifted into a new *Gastalt.* So one of the basic objectives or duties of the person is to understand the existing social order and prepared a new plan for having a better life in future. That is what Wallace called it a more satisfying culture.

Wallace also suggested that his idea of revitalization implies an "organismic analogy"[6] While making an attempt to draw this conceptual idea he cited the nature of the working and composition of human body. He was of the view that like the system of the working of the human organ the human society is also a definite kind of humanism. As in the nature of the working of the human body the character of the society is determined not only by the pattern of the behavior of the persons and groups but also by the cells and organs in which the persons are composed. The successful working of the nature of society as an integrated organism is entirely depends on the net work of intercommunication. He wrote, "A corollary of the organismic analogy is the principle of the homeostasis; that a society will work, by means of co-ordinate actions(including 'cultural' action) by all or some of its parts to preserve its own integrity by maintaining a minimally fluctuating, life supporting matrix for its individual members and will, under stress, take emergency measure to preserve the constancy of the matrix".[7] He also said that the working of the social organism is always associated with stress either as some part or whole. The degree of the stress may be more or less but it always disturbed the natural process of the social organism. In this respect it is also suggested that if every person in the society could maintain a mental image of the society and its culture at all levels of the system the degree of the stress would be able to reduce. At the same time they have to maintain their own body and its behavioral regularities. This 'mental image' was called by Wallace as 'mazeway'.[8] He wrote, "The mazeway is nature, society and culture, personality and body of image, as seen by one person".[9] He further said that the 'mazeway' is an important parameter in the maintenance of social life. But when the mazeway does not lead to action to reduce the level of stress the people in the society have to choose between the maintaining the present mazeway and tolerating the stress or changing the mazeway for an attempt to reduce the stress. Wallace further said that "changing the mazeway involves changing the total '*Gastalt*' of his image of self, society and culture of nature and body, and ways of action.[10] Such type of efforts to change in mazeway for the reduction of the degree of stress in a more effective way may be treated as an attempt for revitalization and the nature of involvement of the masses in such action is called 'revitalisation movement'.[11] From this angle it is said that revitalization movements, mainly because of its idea of revolutionary changes have given a notable contribution for social disruption. And this phenomenon itself is also a great opportunity to the members of the society to replace the old social pattern of behavior with new one. It is also observed that unrest is imperative because without discontent with the present situation there can be no plan internally motivated and directed intentional change. Indeed, the revitalization movement is a recurrent feature in human history.

Katherin Watier wrote, "Revitalisation movements appear out of social situations where groups are faced with the loss of identity and threat of cultural extinction."[12] He was also of the view that such type of mass involvements reaction is a kind of strong protest against the acculturation steps faced by the dominant social power.[13] It is also suggested that one of the basic objectives of the revitalization movements is to make an attempt to give deliverance from deprivation and elimination of foreign domination. The idea is based on the concept of nativism which always aimed to purge the society from the influence of unwanted aliens and elements of foreign origin. In this area there is a slight difference between 'revivalism' and 'revitalization' movements in their approach and objectives. The revivalist movement basically aimed to revive the old tradition from the position of unmoving stage and return to a former era of happiness, to restore in a golden age, to revive a previous condition of social virtue. It only emphasized the institution of customs, value and even aspects of nature which are thought to have been in the mazeway of previous generation but are not now present.[14] Whereas in the case of revitalization movements the basic objective is to strengthen and reactivate the previous social, cultural and religious values which are dominated by the foreign origin. From this angle it can be suggested that the revitalization movements, apart from the objective of giving deliverance from deprivation also made an attempt to give a new interpretation of the human condition based on traditional cultural and religious values which are under sever stress from the colonial conquest and intense class of racial exploitation.

In regard to the religious revitalization movements it is said that it is "an attempt to revive religious tradition through practical innovations and new expression of traditional piety".[15] While giving the observation Rodney Stark and William Sin Bainbridge made an attempt to define the religious organization with a different identity and tried to give a value judgment in each movement. They were of the view that a religion must be based on some 'supernatural assumption' to distinguish it from secular thought. So religion involves system of general compensators based on supernatural assumption. The term 'compensator' was again interpreted by Henry Fielding as the persons rewarded for their involvement or those elements not immediately apparent. He was of the view that the religion organizations as defined by Stark and Bainbridge like 'Church' as a conventional religious organization, 'Sect' as a deviant religious organization with traditional beliefs and practices and 'Cult' as a deviant religious organization with moral belief and practices also can be seen as a revitalization movements because these religious organizations, in one way or other aimed to bring a revolutionary change with a new innovation and expression. However they do not attempt to make a fundamental change in tradition or incooperate radically new beliefs. One of the basic aims of revitalization movement is not to produce new religion rather they reaffirm the old tradition. In this respect Wallace said that "religious revitalization movements generally begin with a supernatural appearance to a single individual who comes to the realization that the old way of life is passing away".[16] His idea of immediate need of the appearance of a supernatural individual indicates the importance of a leader who can give direction for having a successful revitalization movements. The said leader, as Wallace has mentioned, should have possessed the character of 'genuinely charismatic' personality. It is also an accepted view that origin of the religious movement or any type of religion was linked to a particular condition of the society in which they were born. In this respect, though it is not required to go into detail about the nature of religion, it can be observed that religion is the primary means of communication in the society and also embodied the fundamental values of the life. So when there is a state of crisis caused by oppression, deprivation or frustration all the hopes for betterment are expressed in mythical-ritual symbols[17]. In such situation the appeals of the charismatic personality gives a very good and effective social and ethical prescription to the participants who are expecting a total regeneration in the cultural and religious life of the society. But a practical vision for religious revitalizing in any society would be a mere attempt of an individual until and unless it is successfully communicated to other members of the society. Therefore the leader of a charismatic personality should have a clear vision for an alternative mazeway reformation against the existing cultural dissonance caused by the social stratification, economic exploitation, foreign domination and moral decay of the present leadership.[18]

The religious revitalization movement or any type of social movements for that matter has been generally observed to go through certain procedural stages. If these stages are not fulfilled very effectively the movement cannot achieve its basic aim to transform the society. It is also noticed that sometimes the movements are not able to complete the cycle of these stages. Many factors were responsible for the outbreak of such phenomenon. It may be caused by the strong resistance or suppression by the existing force and on the other hand it may be due to the disappointing performance of the leader who failed to attract or retain a sufficient membership. Wallace identified three major historical stages as a pre-movement phase of a religious revitalization movement. They are 1. Steady State, 2.Period of individual stress, 3.Period of cultural distortion.

Steady State

This is the period of social conformity, acceptance of common set of values, the fulfillment of individual needs and the resolution of social conflicts. However even during this period also there are so many ideas of likes and dislikes to the existing status quo of the system in the social life of the people. But such things were not openly manifested to a visible point. Though it is not come out openly the degree of the increasing level of stress was in the minds of the people. Wallace said that the chronic stress within the society varies within tolerable limits. Some are severe but still tolerable stress may remain general in the population. So to maintain equilibrium in the social and natural environment a gradual modification or even rapid substitution techniques for satisfying some needs may be occurred. He further said that the technique for satisfying other needs should not seriously interfeered the interest of other needs. Therefore as the beginning of the process of revitalization movement a satisfactory adaptation situation should be created to maintain the natural environment of the different needs of the social group.

Period of individual stress

Changes and developments are the natural phenomenon of the society. These changes were brought forth by social, economic, or technological innovations and external forces. On the other hand it also produced a serious effect to the equilibrium in the mindset of the people. A sharp competition between the existing social behavior and new trend was developed in the minds of the people. Such type of conflicting competition laid a foundation for having a situation to increase the level of the degree of individual stress.[19] The experience of the increasing in the degree of stress among the individual members of the population was mainly due to the decreasing efficiency of certain reduction technique mainly created by the increase of social competition and ethnic conflict. Wallace wrote, "While the individual can tolerate a moderate degree of increased stress and still maintain the habitual way of behavior, a point is reached out which some alternative way must be considered. Initial consideration by a substitute way is likely, however to increase stress because it arouses anxiety over the possibility that the substitute way will be even less effective than the original, and that it also actively interfere with the execution of other ways"[20]. Such type of atmosphere has increased the degree of social disruption and decreased the level of individual satisfaction. A large number of individuals are placed under intolerable stress by the failure of the system to accommodate the satisfaction of their needs. Ultimately a situation was developed to put the traditional methods and its value judgment to test because individual desire to get more satisfactory needs and help. This stage is identified as the second phase for the outbreak of revitalisation movement.

Period of cultural distortion

The third phase for having a stage for the outbreak of revitalisation movement is directly related with the outcome of the failure of the internal mechanism to reduce the increasing levels of anxiety. It is mentioned that when the members of the society have a bitter experience of the failure to reduce the increasing level of anxiety, they began to look towards the rising level of stress. This evolving process from the first and second phases is regarded as a period of cultural distortion. It is also said that when the members find their situation intolerable or little hope of relief by the use of the available culturally sanction means, they immediately turn to "idiosyncratic or systematically deviant means"[21]. This phase is characterized as the stage of "disillusionment, apathy, cultural deterioration and internal factionalism" [22]. Wallace also said that prolong experience of stress and failure of need satisfaction techniques to reduce anxiety have produced different response by different people. He further observed that rigid people prefer to tolerate high level of chronic stress rather than make systematic adaptive changes in the mazeway. More flexible people try to change their limited mazeway by reducing stress or substitution of mazeway elements[23]. He further said that the increasing stress and anxiety have compelled the people to turn towards the psycho dynamically regressive innovations. Such type of regressive response made a fundamental foundation for the increase of socially dysfunctional customs like alcoholism, extreme passivity and indolecense organized crimes, disregard of kinship and sexual harassment irresponsibility in the public officials, state of depression and self approach excessive corruption of officials, mob, violence, sabotage, vandalism etc. Merton called such type social situation as 'anonei'[24] period. Such situation leads to the distortion of cultural fabric by the institutionalization of such socially dysfunctional customs. And automatically the internal distorted culture like lack of elements in harmonious relationship and growth of ideas mutually inconsistent and interfering leads to the continuous rise of the degree of the level of stress. Wallace wrote, "as the inadequacy of existing way of acting to reduce stress becomes more and more evident, and as the internal incongruities of the mazeway all perceived, symptoms of anxiety over the loss of meaningful way of life also become evident: disillusionment with the mazeway, and apathy towards problem of adaptation, set in" [25].

The failure to reduce the level of anxiety ultimately produced the increase of the degree of the level of stress among the people. The emergence of such type of situation in a given society is very dangerous and this deterioration process is not checked or stop in a right time it would lead to the death of the society. Factional disputes may be nibble away areas and segments of population, death rate may be increased birth rate may be decreased; society may be defeated in war, its population dispersed and its customs suppressed. But these terrible events can be forestalled or at least postponed by a revitalization movement. Wallace was also of the view that such movements are always associated with the concept of religious nature in character. He further said that revitalization movements of any type must perform six major tasks. They are also again divided into two parts i.e. movement period and post movement period. The tasks of the movement period are 1.Prophetic formulation of code, 2.Communication of code, 3. Organization, 4. Adaptation, 5. Cultural Transformation and 6. Routization.

1. *Prophetic formulation of code* —Wallace used to call this task as the stage of the 'Mazeway reformulation'[26]. It is a fact that revitalisation movement launched when there is an adaptive social

response whereby the past and present values, costumes, beliefs which produce dissonance arising from the distortions that exist between them are analysed and recombined into new synthesis, a new mazeway or a new gestalt[27]. Wallace also pointed out that reformulation of mazeway is to depend on a "restructuring of elements and sub systems which have already attained currency in the society, which are known to the person who is to become the prophet or leader"[28]. This phase is very important stage because during this period a combination between the existing value and new conceptual idea emerged side by side and it created an opportune moment to realize the relationship between this two. These moments are called 'inspiration and revelation.'[29] The idea of such type of opportune moment and the concept of reformulation is always grow as an initial form in the mind of a single person who is accepted as a guide or leader or prophet by the society later on. It is also mentioned that every religious revitalisation movements always started with hallucinatory vision which is conceived to a single individual. In this stage the leader or prophet will act as a supernatural being and explained the society's trouble as being entirely or partly a result or violation of certain rules. Apart from this visionary promises are made to the individuals and society for revitalisation. Wallace called such type of leader as 'dreamer'. He said that the dream expresses "1. The dreamer's wish for a satisfying parental figure (supernatural, guardian spirit content), 2. World destruction fantasies (apocalyptic millennial content), 3. Feeling of guilt and anxiety(the moral content) and 4.longing for the establishment of an ideal state of stable and satisfying human and supernatural relations (the restitution fantasy or utopian content)."[30] In a sense this period is a formative stage of the dreamers to demonstrate a visionary experience for a radical change in the personality, to assume a new role in society, to give a new plan devises for reorganizing society and proposes a new order that promises a new meaning and purpose for living. In fact at this stage the leader or prophet arises the issues why things have gotten so bad and how to make better. Thus at the initial stage of the religious revitalization movements the dreamers always made a successful attempt to convince the members of the society by presenting a new mazeway *Gestalt* with more or less innovation in detail of content.

Communication of code

This is the second phase of the religious revitalisation movement. At this stage the dreamer who reformulates a new mazeway in their mind has transmitted directly to the group for deliberation. They undertook to preach their revelation to the people in a more evangelistic and messianic spirit. From this nature they became a prophet or leader and they tells the people the code in order to attract converts. It is also mentioned that in the nature of his preaches the leader or prophet always carry two fundamentals motifs *i.e*, to bring converts under the care and protection of certain supernatural being and to give material benefit to the society from the identification with some definable new cultural system.[31] No doubt 'communication' phase is a very important stage for a successful religious revitalisation movement because at this period only the opportunity for the participation and involvement of the masses was able to enjoy by the society. And a successful mass involvement would be achieved only when the visionary mental blue print for social, cultural and religious change is transmitted successfully by the leader or prophet to other members of the society.

Organisation

From this phase, the final preparation for a religious revitalization movement starts. After having a successful communication with the other members of the society through their visionary mental blue print for a drastic change in every aspect of the life of the society, the converts are attracted and began to feel the immediate need to organize for the materialization of the new objective. Wallace classified the nature of the convert crowd in the several categories. According to his observation "some undergo hysterical seizures induced by suggestion in a crowed situation, some experienced in ecstatic vision in private circumstances, some are convinced by more or less rational arguments, and some by considerations of expediency and opportunity."[32] Whatever the differences in their outlook they are all in favour of change on the line of preaching of the prophet or leader. So in order to launch an effective religious revitalization movement a small clique of special disciple is formed to carry out the new mazeway gastalt of the dreamer. Ultimately the organizational work to implement the proposed changes was carried on under the guidance of the dreamer who was always possessed the quality of charismatic leadership.

Adaptation

Just after the accomplishment of all the first three phases the leader or prophet took the people towards the process for the materialisation of their objective. At this stage the nature and character of the movement began to turn towards the revolutionary activities. And ultimately they began to face steep resistance from the existing social behavior. Since the revolutionary character of the movement aimed for a drastic change in the given environment its activities may create a situation to perceive a threatening atmosphere to those who have power within the larger society in particular. In order to face any type of resistance from the personalities of the established order of the existing system the movement has to use various strategies of adaptation without disturbing the basic ideological objective. The type of strategies may be doctrinal modification, political and maneuver and force. The strategies of adaptation may be suited or not in the existing conditions but it should be imperative of the organizational movement. Wallace said that in the midst of the criticism and negative nature from the existing outlook the leader or prophet is able to modify the original doctrine by adopting the tools of adding or eliminating method so that it makes the new doctrine more acceptable to the life of the society. In this stage the only problem to be tackle by the organizers is the counter hostility from the unbelievers. So they have to shift from cultivation of the ideal to combat against the unbelievers. This stage is the most crucial period because it involves the question of the success and failure of the proposed revitalization movement.

Cultural transformation

This is a positive phase where the vision of the reformer or prophet is acknowledged by the members and transformed into as the daily behavior of the people. The acceptance of new religious concept and practices with its various injunctions signalized the degree of the reduction of the personnel deterioration symptoms of individuals. The enthusiastic action programmed of the organized group also made a significant contribution in the process of the extensive cultural changes in the behavior of the society. Thus the acceptance of new code and to welcome the system of cultural transform is a positive sign for the institution of new culture and religious outlook.

Routinization

This is a stage in which the function of the religious revitalization movement shifts from the innovation to the maintenance of the new cultural tradition. Once the process of the new cultural transformation as per the vision of the leader or prophet is fully accomplished or well understood by the members of the society the organizational character began to change from the original position. And they have started to monitor the degree of the effective in reducing stress generating situation of the society and take responsibility to maintain the doctrine and to perform the ritual. However since many of these changes do not come easily, the leadership needs to monitor and encourage the followers to complete the process by integrating the new values, beliefs and behavior into the cultural norms of the people.

New steady state

This is the last phase of the cyclistic process of a successful religious revitalization movement. Once the cultural transformation is successfully accomplished and the organizational activities have been routinised, a new steady state may be said to exist. No doubt the nature, patterns and outlook will probably different from early steady state. But the final outcome from these long revitalization movements would bring a totally new set of outlook from the period of cultural distortion.

This process ultimately rendered a sizeable contribution to their efforts to perpetuate their own culture. On the other side this process may be taken as an explicit endeavour to realize that there are cultures of their own. The strong tendency to foster and maintain their distinctive cultural identity and to realize the threatening tone from the other culture is regarded by some writers as an impact of gradual development and urbanization forces. Whatever may be but it can be observed that every ethnic group can maintain their viable identity only when they have got the sign and symbols and their underlying values. Royce said that these are the points to the promotion for a distinctive identity.[33]

It has already mentioned above about the failure of the decrease of stress and anxiety which have led for the outbreak of a revitalization movement under the guidance of a supernatural element. But the nature of the outbreak of the movement was not of the same ideological pattern. The movement occurred according to different social and religious circumstances. Anthony Wallace had categorized these circumstances under four major schools of thought. They are: 1. Absolute deprivation theory, 2.Acculturation theory. 3. Social revolutionary theory and 4. Social deprivation theory.

The absolute deprivation theory- The material developments in the social life of a nation had produced a serious problem of class differences *i.e.* high material standard and low material standard. Such type of differences between high and low condition is termed as absolute material deprivation. And the low material standard of living condition gives room for the growth of dissatisfaction to the existing status quo. And its accumulating efforts finally led to the adoption of a revolutionary ideology. However Wallace was of the view that mere material deprivation in any given society cannot be an inevitable reason for the outbreak of revolt or any type of revitalization movement. He said, "Social movements sometimes occurred not in the least fortunate class or nation, nor in the most, but in a middle station."[34]

The acculturation theory

The acculturation is the resultant impact of the contact between the two cultures. But normally such type of phenomenon always occurred among the tribal people after having contact with the culture of more civilized nation. To give pressure or interference to the existing cultural life is one of the characteristic features of the acculturation process. In a way it can be treated as a kind of cultural colonialism activities of a more civilized nation. Naturally it produced a serious implication in their social and cultural life and finally it produced a state of 'cultural shock'[35] among the tribal people. At this stage the people had an experienced of a sort of 'collective historical syndrome characterized by ecstatic'[36]. Such type of acculturation process also rendered a contributing factor for the outbreak of fanatical social movements. Wallace wrote, "The nature of the trauma inflicted by the higher civilization upon the lower may be conceived as the imposition of a competitive way of life, or as the requirement of an unfamiliar pattern of culture, or simply as interference with tradition.."[37]

The social revolutionary theory

This theoretical concept and idea is formulated on the basic principle of Marxian interpretation. The researchers working in the tradition of social criticism and analysis always considered any movements launched by the people as an expression of social protest by disadvantage classes or groups. Therefore they were of the view that all the different types of movement in Europe and other parts of Asia were regarded as a premature popular protest against the oppressive social condition. Their attempt was no doubt a super nationalistic effort to overturn the social order. But they lack the spirit to challenge the existing resistance very effectively with a more rational revolutionary tone. Whatever the case may be but it is also suggested that the social revolutionary process of these movements has created a situation for a more effective revolutionary change in the given society.

The relative deprivation theory

One of the basic features of any type of revitalization movement was to give awareness and recognize the influence of the local situation as a determining factor in the degree of the increasing discrepancy between the levels of aspiration and levels of realization. Such type of situation is regarded as 'relative deprivation' stage. The outbreak of any type revitalization movement was a resultant effect of the conflict between old and new social behavior. Therefore the codes promulgated by the leader or the prophet as a content of the movement was always determined by the cultural materials locally available at the time. The materials include the traditional customs of the society and the customs that may be exerting the acculturative pressure. It is also mentioned that even the occurrence, non occurrence and timing of the movement is always determined by the degree of the disillusionment of a significant numbers of members of the society with the way of life now available to them. Even the precise moment at which the movement crystallizes is also very difficult to predict. As a whole individual variability in society greatly influenced the leader or prophet in the process of the movement and so sometimes they are not able to foretell in detail about the contents of the movement. Indeed this motivation of deprivation idea is derived from widespread social and cultural conditions which were the outcome of the awareness of extreme discrepancy.

Within the ideological framework of religious revitalization movement many writers and researchers have made an attempt to identify some movements as the best example of revitalization movements. The 'Ghost Dance' a religious movement launched by the Plains of North America in the year 1890 was one of them. It was purely a religious movement aimed to free themselves from colonial conquest, intense clash or racial exploitation. It was launched under the leadership of Prophet Wovoka. The apocalyptic prophesied of the movement was that the world would be destroyed very soon by fire, flood, and upheavals, and holocaust the intruding whites would be annihilated. However the prophet gave the assurance of salvation for those who participated in certain prescribe dances. He said that this dance would lead the people to pure life, abandoned the white customs and returned of land to the Native Americans. The ritual lasted for five successive days. As a part of ritual danced was performed every night and continued until morning. The ritual was so effective that it swept almost all the areas of the Plains India and activities had even crossed even into the neighbouring cultural areas with various modifications. He members and participants were fully convinced the words of religious prophecy of the leader that through this dance ritual the ancestors and bison herds would return and white people to leave would leave the place.

The movement was based in a very peaceful way. The members and participants in the 'Ghost Dance' ritual had no objective and intention to take up any type of violence activities. But the white people were so much apprehensive to the involvement of the masses in this ritual. They feared that there was every possibilities for the outbreak of an arm uprising. These suspicious directly led to the massacre of over two hundred Sionx men, women and children by the U.S, Army at Wounded Knee. Sitting Bull was killed while making an attempt to resist the arrest. A band of Sionx led by Big Foot was also arrested by the 7th Cavalry on December 28, 1890 while trying to flee into the badland. With this brutal action of the U.S. Military regime the interest of Indian in the Ghost Dance was subsided gradually and thus their vision for the arrival of a new millennium was also ended in the hand of white hostility. However their sincere attempt to revitalize the value of their traditional culture from the undeclared cultural expedition of the foreign elements had produced a very good eye opener contribution for those people who had strong desire to promote and foster the distinctive cultural identity of their own.

The Paliou movement in the Admiralty Island in New Guinea was also another example of the religious revitalization movement. This movement was launched by a group of people called Manus, a coastal people. The basic aim of the movement was to establish a new religious, economic and political system to maintain their own identity. The movement was launched under the leadership of Paliou, a prophetic leader of the community. The movement sought for a greater degree of economic and political sovereignty which they had not enjoyed under either Japanese or Australian administration. Therefore with this sole objective the movement brought many changes in their religious outlook, political and economic patterns.

They also proposed new standard of family organization. Thus they had made a complete innovation in the whole cultural and social life of the Meues. Indeed the Paliau movement aimed to bring the native people into the mainstream of world cultural development. However the existing administrative authority had a critical eye on the activities of Paliau and his movement. Accordingly the members of the movement had faced a number of resistances from the administration. As a result of this they have got a lot of setback in the course of their activities. But in due course of time they were able to achieve their desire objective and certain degree of self respect and self-supporting opportunity. Ultimately such type of positive development led to the establishment of a new link with the rest of the modern world.

Apart from these two movements they have also made an attempt to justify the Tai Ping rebellion and Boxer Uprising in China as an example having the character and nature of revitalization movement. Many writers' and researchers on the history and culture of Africans also tried to identify some of their mass involvement activities as the revitalization movement. The concept of 'Black Nationalism' which was developed among the Black Americans by emphasizing their African origin and identity, their pride in being black, was also claimed as a good example of revitalization movement. It is mentioned that although it is very difficult to trace the history of the exact origin of the 'Black Nationalist Movement' the protest against the brutal and dehumanising[38] condition of slavery may be treated as the beginning of the growth of the idea of nationalism among the Black Americans. It is said that 'Black Nationalist movement' as an organized forum began to appear under the leadership of one Paul Cuff (1759-1817), a black sea captain.[39] And between 1811 and 1815 he made the first attempt to establish a black American colony in Africa by transporting several dozen people there. Then in the early part of the 20th century the idea of a Pan American Movement emerged. It was followed by the formation of the Universal Negro Improvement Association (UNIA) under the leadership of Marcus Garvey. His objective was to see the development of black capitalist enterprises. But his movement was failed. Again in the beginning of 1930, the idea of African oriented movement emerged and under the leadership of Elijaha Muhammad the concept of the 'Nation of Islam' popularly known as Black Muslim was formulated. The motive behind the conceptual framework was to establish a separate nation outside the United States of America or autonomy within the U.S.A.

The Zeliangrong Movement in Manipur which was regarded as significant mass involvement activities having a distinctive nature of millenarian character can also be treated as a good example of religious revitalization movement in Manipur. It was launched under the prophetic leadership of Jadonang. The basic objective at the beginning of the movement concentrated to the issue of the revitalization the traditional religious and cultural practices and concept against the gradual process of the religious colonization of the Christian Missionary activities. In order to materialize their basic aim and objective he reactivated the religious concept of "Supreme God'(Tingkao Ragwang or Ragwang) and through this platform he made a successful attempt to bring the Zeme, Rongmei and Liangmei different group of people of the same ethnic line together under the roof of a single nomenclature 'Zeliangrong'. After having a successful attempt to bring a social cohesiveness among the different groups of people he started to give strong emphasis for the promotion and maintenance for a distinctive cultural and religious identity. His prophetic message was so powerful that it arouses the masses and ultimately it became a great threat to the existence of the colonial administrators particularly in their attempt to establish a religious colony in the tribal belt areas in Manipur. Then gradually the tone of the movement also began to change by adding certain ideas of political element. The demand for the establishment of 'Naga Raj' had produced a mix impact in the existing social, religious, political and colonial administration. When the prophetic leader asked for the establishment of a separate political identity the people warmly received it as a new gift which was not at all in their mind. On the other hand the colonial masters took it as a great threat to their existence. Therefore they prepared to take an opportune time to suppress the movement. While this was the situation an unfortunate incident took place in which five Meitei betel leave traders were killed by the people of Jadonang. The colonial officers took it as an opportune time to crush the movement. Accordingly he was arrested as a criminal for killing the Meitei traders and with this allegation he was put to death in the year 1932. After his death the activities of the movement was carried on by a girl named Gaidinliu popularly known as Rani Gaidinliu. But the ideas and objective behind the movement was a great siginificant in the process for the revitalization of the traditional social, cultural and religious life of the Zeliangrong people. Ultimately it became an eye opener to those people who desire to promote and foster their traditional way of life in a more distinctive and scientific character.

NOTES

1. Vittorio Lanternari, Nativitic, *Socio Religions Movement: A Reconsideration (Comparative Studies in Society of History,* vol. 16 no. Supl. 1974) p. 484.
2. *Ibid.*
3. Loren Von Stein. *History of Social Movement in France 1989-1950*, 1950.
4. Anthony F.C. Wallace: - Revitalization Movement (*American Anthropologist,* New Series Vol. 58, No.2, April, 1956), p. 265.
5. *Ibid.*
6. *Ibid.*
7. *Ibid.*
8. *Ibid.* p. 266.
9. *Ibid.*
10. *Ibid.* p. 267.
11. *Ibid.*
12. Katherin Walin, *Revitalization Movements and their Characteristic,* February, 23, 1998.
13. *Ibid.*
14. James Meovey, The Ghost Dance Religion Bureau of American Ethnology, Annual Report, Washington, 1992-93 Quoted by Wallace, *Ibid.* p. 267.
15. Rodney Stark and Willian Sim Bainbriage, *A Theory of Religion* (New York) Petan Lay, 1987.

16. Renneth D. Tollefron, Titen epistle of religion revitalization, *Biblical Theology Bulletin*, Winter 2000, p. 7.
17. Vittorio Lanterney, *op.cit.*, p. 487.
18. Kenneth D. Tolletson, *op.cit.*, p.5.
19. *Ibid*, p.1.
20. A.F.C. Wallace, *op.cit.*, p. 269.
21. *International Encyclopedia of Social Science*, vol.11-12, p. 76.
22. Kenneth D. Tollefson, *op.cit.*, p.2.
23. A.F.C. Wallace, *op.cit.*, p.269.
24. Merton Robert K:- Social Structure and Anonei (Pub. in Social Theory and Social Structure, Rev. and End. End, Glccoe Ill. Free-Press) pp.131-160.
25. A.F.C. Wallace, *op.cit.*, p.270.
26. *Ibid.*
27. Kenneth D. Tollefson:- *op.cit.*, p. 2.
28. A.F.C. Wallace, *op.cit.*, p.2.
29. *Ibid.*
30. *Ibid.*
31. *Ibid.* p.22.
32. *Ibid.*
33. Royce Anya, *Ethnic Identity; Strategies of Diversity Bleomiylon in India*. University Arn, 1982.
34. *International Encyclopedia of Social Science*, vol. 11-12, p.77.
35. *Ibid.*
36. *Ibid.*
37. *Ibid.*
38. Black National, *A Revitalizatic Movement.*
39. *Ibid.*

2

Primary Religion in Manipur

Religion is the life of the people and it always plays a great contributory role in the society by giving a solid foundation in the process of the establishment of unity, cohesiveness and moral discipline among the people. The term 'religion' is defined as "a set of beliefs concerning the universe specially when considered as the creation of a super human agency or agencies usually having a moral code for the conduct of human affairs". Many writers make an attempt to define the term from different perspectives. Some says that it is a belief in super human controlling power. Others are of the view that it is a particular system of faith and worship. Indeed, as the term covers a wide ranging areas of concept of philosophy it is very difficult to give a clear definition of the term 'religion'. The term religion is derived from the Latin word *religo* or *religonis* which means obligation, bond, reverence.[1] From this definitions it can be suggested that it is a concept which binds the people to maintain social discipline. Still many writers with great difficulties tried to define the basic essence of the term religion in various ways. In fact the concept of the term brings the people in a core of belief and expressed publicly in ritual form. It is also a specific and institutionalized set of beliefs and practices generally agreed upon by a number of persons or section. Analysing from the conceptual framework of 'faith' or 'belief' it is also observed that religion is the system of worship of god by men with a code of moral, spiritual and social behaviour dealing with god and society.[2] In another sense religion may be treated as an important social element as it involves in all the common plight of people at all time irrespective of sex, age and status within the society. Therefore apart from its contribution of religious insight and knowledge it also binds all the people to the dictates of the social values and social groups through the religious concept of supernatural and part of salvation. Such type of phenomenon provides an opportunity to understand the value of collectivism and social harmony. From this angle the religion is observed as "both intensely personal and intensely social."[3]

E.B.Tylor explained religion as "a system of beliefs and practices, found in every culture that formalizes the conception of the relation between man and his environment. It helps to explain different and seemingly inexplicable events. Religion embodies the idea of supernatural power and personified supernatural forces."[4] He further said that "religion organizes a group's member in a condition of solidarity and gives a broad base to social interection[5]. Emile Durkheim was of the view that religion understood sets of beliefs and practices to enable individuals who engaged in them to form share and social identity. James Martincau said religion is the belief in an even living god, that is in a 'Divine Mind and Will' ruling the 'Universe' and holding moral relations with mankind. Herbert Spencer wrote, religion is the recognition that all this are manifestation of 'Power' which transcends our knowledge. Sigmund Freud (1856-1939) emphasized the importance of religious behavior in helping people to vent anti social anxieties in a manner that does not threaten their place within the group. Their nature of observation was regarded by Russel T. Cutcheon as 'functional approach'[6] because their attempt was to deploy the role of religion in helping individuals and communities to reproduced themselves. Therefore they were of the view that perhaps they believed that the basic duty of the religion is 'to help to satisfy human needs'. Even Karl Marx (1818-1883) also makes attempt to observe from the line of the concept of functional approach. He defined religion a pacifier of the sense of pain and alienation of deadened and oppressed people. Simultaneously it also prevented them from doing something about their lot in life.

Frederick Engel, by analysing from the framework of the materialistic point of view, defined religion as a "fantastic reflection in man's minds of those external forces which control their daily life, a reflection in which the terrestrial forces assume the form of supernatural forces".[7] The people who shared the approach of Marxism and Leninism always considered religion as a 'historically transient phenomenon of social consciousness and shows the main factors that determine its existence at different stages of society's development.'[8] They also took it as a means to strengthen and perpetual man's dependence on external forces and doom his passiveness, holding down his creative potential. They strongly believed that religious diverts the working people from active participation in the struggle for changing the world rather it impedes the formation of their class consciousness. From this perspective Marxists considered religion as 'opium for people'.

Whatever it may be religion is an inseparable and indispensible vital part in the life of the people. It plays a great contributing role not only in the process of the proper maintaining in the social and moral behavior among the people but it also helped to the promotion of social equilibrium in the life of the society. Indeed religion is undoubtedly regarded as a life for the promotion of social discipline among the human beings. Some writers interpreted religion as 'historical artifact.'[9] They were of the view that the religion was used by the different social actors to classify certain parts of their social world. Within this conceptual framework religion may be observed as an item of rhetoric used by the group members to sort out their group identities. On the other hand it can also be suggested that the concept and philosophy of religion is used as a driving force in the reform of social abuses. And when it plays the role of driving force for any type of positive changes it has always associated with reaction and oppression. However, though the religion always rendered a significant contribution in the social life of the people still it is not very clear or rather obscure about the origin of the idea of this term. No doubt various writers make an attempt to advance a theoretical hypothesis based on the relationship between the people and natural objects. They were of the view that the concept of religion emerged out of the constant relationship or communication which was going on between people and natural objects. It is also said that religious belief arose from primitive man's helplessness in the struggle with the force of nature. From this aspect religion may be taken as the deepest and most engrossing form of human activities. In this long process of the development of human civilization the people have enjoyed various types of religious philosophy, concept, practice and approach. It is mentioned that in every religion there is some sort of awareness of what is called divine and some sort of response to this divinity. But the question is where the divine is and what sort of response is primarily made to it. It is also suggested that these quarries may be solved if the principles and concept is to be analysed from three major aspects *i.e.*, sacramental, prophetic and mystical.

The primitive character of religion is treated as a sacramental type of religious practices. Under this conceptual framework the people always sought divine in inanimate physical things like wood, the totem animals etc. It was believed that these sacred things are the manifestation or habitation of some god or spirit. This type of religious concept is also known as the idea of 'fetishism'. However this does not mean that the inanimate things itself are responded to as divine. But these material things perhaps might have been taken as symbol of the divine rather than as its direct embodiment. The sacramental religious practice is regarded as 'an outward and visible sign of an inward and spiritual grace'.[10] It is further said that "where sacramentalism is strong in a monotheistic religion, the natural tendency is to take everything in natural as a divine manifestation."[11] Such type of the religious practices of sacramentalism is found in the character of primitive religion.

In the nature of the prophetic religion the concept of divine is believed to be manifested in human society and in their history. It is not an undeniable fact that nature issues from the divine and is under the divine control. But it is also believed that the divine reality is to be discovered in great historical events like the destruction of cities, rise and falloff empires, the escape of people from bondage etc.[12] It is the religious impression that in such great historical events the hands of the god is seen. God encountered these events through his messengers; the prophet who could reveal the nature of the God in their utterances. From this point of view the nature of the prophetic religion is also observed as a "revelation" that it stresses the word as the medium of contact with the divine[13]. The response of the prophetic religion is based on the co-ordination with the chief form in which the divine is apprehended. The acceptance of divine message and obedience to the command and exhortations it contains perhaps may be the chief forms. Indeed, the idea of "faith" is the supreme virtue in this prophetic religion. Therefore since "faith" is the central for prophetic religion the idea of affirmation and confession always plays an important role.[14]

The idea and nature of mystical religion is quite different from the first two types of religion. The mystical experience is the main centre of this religion. The nature of this religious experience is always associated with an individual who always considered him pervaded and transformed by the divine. And they always tried to identify themselves with the divine personality. So they considered all the practices and principles of other types of religion as paltry substitute. They also dismissed the concept of other religion as superior or inferior. Their immediate identification with the divine is the supreme religious character. So, the individual, because of this condition, utilized their energy within the core of their belief and concentrate their time on an ascetic and contemplate discipline. It is mentioned that "all mystical experience and the divinity it reveals are often regarded as ineffable, not to be expressed in human language, hence, mystics tends to reject all doctrinal formulations as inadequate."[15]

But Frank Byron Jevons classified religion only from two angles. According to his observation there are only two religious principles. One is religion enacted by the founders to supersede certain existing religious and other one is not being enacted by the authority of any founder but being practice as a matter of custom and tradition.[16] This two types of religious approaches are termed, first one as a 'Positive religion' and other one as 'Customary religion.' He put the religion like Christianity, Buddhism, Jainism, Islam religion etc. to the category of the 'Positive religion' as these religions were founded under the certain religious principles of a founder. In the practice of 'Customary religion' the role of the institution, may be either religion or social, always plays an important part. On the other hand these two institutions may be observed as the two faces of the same coin because religious institution also has their social side. In this line Jevons strongly asserted that religious worship is a public institution because the gods are the gods of the community. While the process is going on all the members of the community have to perform the religious rites in a mode of united way. From this point of observation it can be suggested that though the idea of religion conceived to meet the need of individual but in due course of time its root lie in society and social processes. On the other side religion may be observed as an essential integrating force which helps in bringing a social cohesiveness in a given society.

It has already mentioned above about the close relationship between the religion and day to day life of the human beings. Indeed, religion may be taken as a strong moving force in the developmental process of the human being. And every individual and society is moving through a religious platform of their own belief. From this aspect it has rightly said that "there are no people without a religion" [17]. After giving so many analytical observations the writers finally squeezed the types of religion into two, i.e. positive and customary religion or modern and primitive religion. Modern religion is defined as a world religion and primitive religion is observed as a religion based on the indigenous faith which has developed among those people who believed in and practice them[18]. Such type of religion is also categorized as "native cult."[19] But E.B.Taylor who was regarded as the father of anthropology used to call such type of religion as' animism'. His idea and observation was based on the belief in the spiritual beings which was practiced among the savages. Taylor used to call the primitive people as 'savage'. But his concept of traditional religion was criticized by many writers. People like Andrew Lang, a Scottish folklorist, Wilhelm Schmidt and Dr. Harold Turner a

Presbyterian theologies of New Zealand strongly refuted the concept of animism. Rather they strongly emphasized that such type of religion should be termed as 'primordial monotheism' among the primitive people. By giving justification to their observation they have pointed out the concept of High God, a benign creator of the universe who was regarded as the legislator of moral order which is found among the primitive people. Therefore according to them the religious concept of primitive people should be replaced by that term 'Primal Religion'. On the basis of this argument they claimed that the word 'Animism' is a misleading term. Dr. Turner had categorically asserted all the religions which were existed prior to the universal religion or modern religion or positive religion should be categorized as 'Primal Religion'. On the basis of this observation it is also said that "the primal religion covers all the features of the indigenous faith or the tribal religion. An indigenous faith implies an ancient root and cultural heritage, the present consciousness and future continuence."[20] It is further said that "Primordial religion meaning a religion with a primordial existence; existing since the beginning of time. Primodiality is basic to any religion which is based on a myth of creation which ascribes to the 'Supreme Being' as creator of universe, men and all living beings"[21]. Whatever may be particularly on the conceptual interpretation of the nature of the traditional religious practices but so far the religious beliefs among the indigenous of the hill areas of the north eastern states of India is concerned it is quite evident about the existence of the concept of polytheism with a strong belief in the 'Supreme God'. The indigenous people of this area strongly believed the concept of Supreme Being as the creator and 'Almighty God'. On the basis of this belief they were able to maintain a cultural heritage and social solidarity.

After having a long experience of the concept and practices of the so called 'modern religion' the people began to look back to the history of religion which existed at a particular time of human civilization. The people used to call it generally as primary or indigenous religion. In a simple sense it can be suggested that the primary religion means the religious principles and practices enjoyed by the people before the coming of the positive religion. At a particular stage of time this type of system formed the majority of the world's religion. However all the primary religions are not in the same form and practice. It is mentioned that every language had practiced various type of primary religion. So different languages brought different religious concept. But in course of time the importance of these religions was gradually deteriorated because of the acceptance of the principles and practices of new religion by the people. Thus the powerful dominating religion brought a drastic change in the whole social and religious outlook of the people. In some areas people makes a successful attempt to bring a synthesis between the primary and new religion. The idea behind this might be to maintain some of the basic religious principles of their traditional religion. Such type of processes on the one hand helps in maintaining of the continuity the traditional religious pictures and on the other side it also shows very good evidence that all the religion cannot be treated as a 'fossilized'[22] remains of the earliest or first religion. Perhaps it may be suggested as a basic foundation for the construction of a more advance religion. Whatever it may be but it is also suggested that the indigenous religion, although it was severely effected may the domination of modern religious colonialism, they rendered a good opportunity to maintain their distinctive identity in this new trend of social life. It is also a fact that all the indigenous religion was more or less closely interrelated with the ways and means of the improving their social conditions and a prosperous life. Particularly in the indigenous religious form of the Asiatic people, the concept is always expressed in ritualized activities by involving the whole community. The relationships with gods and spirit; with fellow's human being and with nature etc. are the key understanding of the view of the people of the Asiatic countries. The concept of supreme god, the idea of ancestor worship, deities presiding over the villages and places are the some important salient features of indigenous religion.[23] The nature and characteristic features of the form of primary religion is always associated with customary practices of the society. Therefore some writers regarded such type of religion as customary religion. In the nature of their practices there were no evidences about the involvement of the initiative of any type of spiritual leadership as was done in the nature of the modern religion. Rather the whole framework of religious concept and practices was centered on the developmental process of the life of their society.

The Primary Religion of Manipur

The indigenous religion of Manipur is based broadly on the two basic concepts. *i.e.* the concept of Supreme God and concept of Ancestor Worship. Within this two religious framework the people of Manipur was able to bring a social discipline in the state. At the same time through this religious philosophy the people were able to promote and foster the cultural heritage and social solidarity.[24] Whatever it may be the idea of the super natural elements is the basic concept of primary religion. This is the firm belief among the people that all the objectives which they could have seen by their naked eyes were the creation of the super natural element is the basic concept of the primary religion. They called it 'Supreme God'. Graham Harvey in his writing claimed that the teaching about a 'God' who created the universe is also one of the basic concepts of indigenous religion.[25] They believed that he is the benevolent and protector of human society. At the same time he was also believed to be the creator of all living and non living objectives. For this he was acknowledged as God monotheist.

The concept of 'Supreme God' was also practiced in other countries of the world. The 'Maoris' a Polynesian people of New Zealand also strongly believed in the concept of supreme god. They called it 'Io', who were believed to live in the highest place of heaven and exercised the ultimate control of all events. The Maori people believed that from his place he produced a dynamic force which has created the universe. This force was known to them as 'Mana' and it is the power of good and evil. The Zulu tribe of Africa also believed to the idea of the Lord-of-the –Sky. In their local language it is called '*iNkosi Yezulu*'. It is said that according to their belief the Lord-of the Sky is the source of both good and evil, kind and generous, but erratic and unpredictable.[26] The Korean people also enjoyed a concept of indigenous religion called 'Synkiyo' means "the religion without a name". In the whole body of this religious concept the Korean people strongly believed the idea of the spirit of heaven which they called it *Hanamin or Hanumin.* They believed that he has a special place in the heaven. It was he who brings sunlight and rain, lightning, draught and disaster. So when disaster came the king used to appeal to *Hanamin* by confessing his own sins and his peoples. It is mentioned that *Hanamin* was the grandfather of '*Tagun*' the aboriginal hero of the Korean people. Indeed, the basic concept of the indigenous religion is focused on the relationship between 'man and cosmos'. Their only believed is that the whole universe is created by a supreme power.

The idea of the creation of universe by a supernatural power was the basic foundation of the concept of the traditional religion of the indigenous people of this place. The people addressed this immortal one as *Tengbanba Mapu* (Supreme Lord of Universe). He was also known as *Guru Sidaba.* Some writers used to write his name as *Kuru Sidaba.*[27] It is said that the word *Guru* might be a derivation form of the word *Kuru.* They further claimed that even this very word '*Kuru*' might have been derived from the word *Kubiba*[28] means to be gracious or to be kind. Whatever the case may be but the people strongly believed that the creation of this universe along with all living objects was the biggest contribution of this immortal one. The creation theory of the indigenous religion has full of romantic with a lot of thrilling activities. It is mentioned that the *Tenbanba Mapu,* after roaming in the space for quite long time have decided to create universe in order to have a place for living beings. Accordingly by using his divine power he produced three powers as his own sons. Later on they were also worshipped by the as divine personalities. They were 1. *Atingkok Sidaba* 2. *Atiya Sidaba* and 3.*Konjil Tingthokpa.*[29] Then he directed his eldest son Atingkok Sidaba to create the universe with the help of his younger brother Atiya Sidaba. It is mentioned that Atingkok Sidaba had expressesd his apprehension to perform the assignment given to him without the blessing of his divine father. To see his uneasiness problem Tengbanba Mapu extended all the possible help by giving all the sacred elements to him.[30] It is also mentioned that in order to get a clear idea in the process of the formation of cosmic world and as a means to get clue he allowed his son to see all the cosmic elements about the nature and characters of the living objectives which were to be introduced just after the completion of the formation of the universe. Thus with all the ideas of his father Atingkok Sidaba was prepared to create all the natural objectives like water, air, fire including hills, rivers etc.

In the process of the creation of the universe there were full of disturbances and obstacles which were deliberately created by the youngest son Konjin Tingthokpa. To see this problem Atiya Sidaba reported the matter to their father Tengbanba Mapu[31]. To see the helpless position of his son Atiya Sidaba and to tackle this problem very effectively Guru Sidaba immediately created a young lady from his ring finger. She was known as Nongthang Leima (the deity of lightning and enchantment). Guru directed her to stop the undesirable action of Konjin Tingthokpa by using all sorts of possible means. But she failed to stop his destructive nature. Then Guru Sidaba again created another young lady called Tampha Awangbi.[32] She was able to divert the attention of Konjin Tingthokpa from his earlier behavior and brought him near her place. While making a successful attempt to win over the attention of Konjin Tingthokpa a dialogue was taking place between them. The nature and style of the dialogue was regarded by many writers as a significant one towards the enrichment in the field of the literature of this place. Taking the opportunity of this situation and in the absence of his destructive action Atiya Sidaba was able to complete his mission very successfully. Thus Atiya Sidaba was able to create the universe according to the desire of their father. Though it is not required going into detail about these events it can be suggested that the creation of living and non living objectives as an important element of the universe was a great work of Tengbanba Mapu. This is the strongest point where the people who believed in the concept of traditional religion paid much special attention. From this belief the people always regarded him as a divine personality. People also believed that he was an omnipresent. The people always thought that this personality is free from any type of natural order like decadence, death, and disappearance. So people thought that he was a supernatural element. Accordingly they placed him in the highest order of the primordial religious concept of Manipur.

The practice of 'Ancestor Worship' is another category of the concept of primary religion of Manipur. It is a type of religions practiced or activities which involved in the worship of, or communication with the souls of a group's ancestors.[33] It is one of the oldest forms of religious activities which were practiced by the people in various forms. It is recorded that the concept of ancestor worship was first introduced in China at the beginning of the Chou dynasty(1122-325 B.C.E.) and it make popularized by 'Confucious'(551-479B.C.E.).[34] The Confucius believed that the parents and elders have to be honoured and respected while they are alive and this idea should be continued even after the death also.[35] William P. Scott defined the ancestor worship as a religious cult based upon the belief that the spirit of the deceased ancestors can influence events in the lives of the living, culturally defied ceremonies or rituals are practiced to honour a family's ancestors (or the ancestors of another designated group such as clan, household etc.)[36] Thus many writers make an attempt to give a philosophical interpretation on the concept of ancestor worship. It is also said that the idea of ancestor worship was developed mainly due to the constant psychological communication between the spirit of death and living beings. It is further mentioned that the inner philosophy of this concept is "to detain the soul of the dying man by offering his favourite dishes, displaying his most cherished possession, praising his noble deeds."[37] Indeed, the idea of ancestor worship perhaps, was emerged just after the flourishment of a settle life. It was also viewed that this idea did not come into existence until the people did gave up their nomad life and the concept of the institution of family was not fully in operational stage. The moment the people had established a settled life, they began to think of their own community. The moment the concept of village community was fully established and attained a settled position the family members of the direct blood relationship began to sever from the community and he became the founder of the family. Thus the idea of ancestor worship begins the moment the settlement period emerges and agricultural life started. It is also said that the people began to remember their ancestors through worshipping with an objective to save and protect themselves from the evil eyes of undesirable elements. Whatever the case may be the concept of ancestor worship occupies a very important position in the concept of the indigenous religion of the people.

The term 'ancestor worship' is known as '*Apokpa Khurumba*'. As was done in other areas this religious ritual is also a very important part of the primary religion of Manipur. Some writers tried to classify it into two parts. One is 'Supreme Being' who was considered as the creator of the whole cosmology and living beings. People called him '*Ipuroi Sidaba*' and another is the forefathers of the family. The people worshipped their forefathers for some specific reasons. One reason is for getting children, the second one is for getting wealth and the other one is for giving good health. In this ritualistic process the people worshipped three predecessors. They are 1.Great Great grandfather 2.Great grandfather and 3 Grandfather. They are called locally as '*Pu Ahal*'(Pu-elder), '*Pu-Yaima*'(Pu-middle) and '*Pu-Atomba*'(Pu-younger). The nature of worship and articles to be used for this ritual is different according to the clan. In Manipur there are seven clans and each clan has their distinctive nature of rites. Even the place of water, firewood, bananaleaf, fish etc. is different according to the colour of the respective clan. The style of the sword is also different according to the clans. Normally people worshipped their ancestors three times according to their desire and requirements. But for every specific reason the time of worship is also different. Thus ancestor worship (Apokpa Khurumba) also played an important role in the developmental process of primary religion in social life of Manipur.

The worship of non - living objectives like trees, plants, rivers, hills and other celestial elements like moon. Planets, stars etc. was also another form of religious concept practiced by the people. Such type of religious belief is also categorized by some writers as the true form of animism. According to them it is a "doctrine which places the source of mental and even physical life of energy independent of or at least distinct from the body."[38] It is also said that the animism is a concept "belief in spiritual beings that are concerned with humane affairs and capable of intervening in them."[39] Sir Edward Bernett Tylor in his celebrated work *'Primitive Culture'* mentioned that animism is the attribution of a soul or spirit to living things and inanimate objects. He was also of the view that in full blown animism nothing is really inanimate; everything is alive with spirit, active or not. Some writers classified animism into three forms viz. 'Necrolatry, Spiritism and Naturism'. Worship of soul of men and animals, manifesting itself above all as worship of the death is in the first category, worship of spiritual beings who are not associated in a permanent way with certain bodies and objects is in the second form and worship of spiritual beings who direct the permanent or periodically recurring phenomena is in the last category.[40]

Whatever the case it may be it also an undeniable fact that in the process of the growth of the society people required many facilities. At a particular stage of time these facilities were provided by the natural objects and non living objectives. In a sense it can be suggested that in every stage of their developmental process, human beings required helps from the natural objectives. It is, indeed, more or less directly related with their own survival in the given environment. Therefore for their survival they used to take help from the natural objectives like trees, plants and animals and non living objectives. At a particular stage of time people always believed that these objectives have possessed some kind of special power. So in order to get certain requirements from them people began to treat them with special care. Thus after passing through many stages these natural elements and objectives became an anthropomorphic god. These natural objectives were animated by the people and started to worship them as an incarnation or representatives of unseen divine elements. Their main objective was to make an alliance between human kind and natural objects to obtain supernatural ally against supernatural foes.[41] Thus under this spontaneous process the people began to worship all sorts of natural objectives including sun, moon, sky etc. which they always considered as an indispensible ally for the growth of meaningful transition from savagery to civilization. Such type of developmental process may be treated as a transition from a natural to an artificial basis. The domestication of animals and cultivation of plants was, indeed an outcome of the establishment of alliance between nature and human beings. So, in course of time the worship of plants and animals gradually became a totem of the people. Thus the unions between nature and human beings have produced a strong impetus in the process of the growth of the society and ultimately this process of union became a part of the customary religion.

Nature of Religious Practices in Cyclistic Ceremonies and Festivals

To observe and perform ceremonies and festivals annually is also an indispensible aspect of the religious life of the society. At the same time it also makes a significant contribution to the growth of the cultural life of the people. Through these ceremonies and festivals the people are able to maintain the distinctive identity and philosophy of their primary religion.

Birth Ceremony

The life cycle of a person begins from the very moment of his/her birth. On the other hand the continuity of the developmental process of the society also maintain with birth of a new children. So to give birth of new children is equally important from the family as well as from the society because they always consider it as a positive sign towards the continuation of the pedigree of the family line. In the larger perspective it is also a positive development in the process of the growth of the society. Therefore from time immemorial the people always took special care to protect the newly born children. The process of special care by the members of the family starts right from the time when the blooming children are inside the womb of their mother. The nature and practices of special attention is made through certain procedure according to their religious belief.

In the case of Manipur also the whole process of the birth of a child is performed under the framework of their traditional religious concept. It is a common belief among the people that the soul is the image of the supreme creator and he sends it in the form of human beings after passing through various stages for twelve months. It is said that the father keeps the soul for two months with him and passes it to mother. She will carry the soul for ten months. During this ten months period the members of the family takes a special care in order not to have any type of undesirable problems like miscarriage or premature death or abortive. To save the blooming child people adop certain rituals like the warded off of evil spirit which is known as '*Lai Amangba* (impure deity). People always belief that this evil spirit caused all sorts of problems during the pregnancy period. After this a special launch is arranged for the mother with a curry chosen by her. It is also believed that this special meal would give more strength to the child who is inside the womb. Then when the stage of the child reach ninth months old another ritual is performed called '*Anam Athou*' and '*Konyai Hunba*'. This ritual is performed to make a free passage at the time of delivery. Then when the stage of pregnancy reach at the last stage the husband again gave a blessing to his wife. This is called '*Anam Athou Kokpa*'. Thus under these procedural religious practices the people strictly perform all norms very carefully and with great attention right from the time of the conceive of child. Even at the delivery time also the people follow all the practices of traditional religion with great attention. All these procedure come to an end just after the father gives the name of the god to the newly bornchild. This particular ritual marks the beginning of the performance of birth ceremony.

The birth ritual is known as *Ipan Thaba*. It is performed either on the fifth or six days from the day of delivery according to the status of sex of the newly born baby. If the child is male the ritual is performed on the sixth day and female on the fifth days from the day of delivery. Some people claim that at a particular period of time this ritual is known as *Yupan Thaba i.e*, giving of intoxicated liquor. The ritual is started from the early morning with the worship of *Ipan Leima* alias *Pithraibi Khongdaibi*. Then it is followed by a ritual called *Thawaimi Konsinba* (calling of soul). After this the food giving ritual is performed. This is locally known as *Chaumba.* During these ritualistic periods the newly born baby is put on a *Yangkok* (winning fan) and the female priest (Maibi) wards off the evil spirit by burning *Khoiju Laikham* a kind of herb available in the state. All these morning rituals are completed with the handing over of child to the mother by the female priest who performes all the religious practices.

Again at evening another birth ritual is performed with the worship of one deity called *Nongdamba Lai* (God of destination). It is generally believed that on the day of *Ipan Thaba* this deity appears to the house of the newly born child and write about his/her future destiny on their forehead. The people take it as a very important moment for the family particularly of the newly born child. Along with this the family also worship other household deities such as *Lainingthou Sanamahi* and *Leimarel Sidabi.* It is said that the worship of Lainingthou Sanamahi was introduced only during the period of King Khagemba in 17th century.[42] Just after the completion of the rituals the priest make the incantation of bow and arrow which is made specially to worship the other deities. It is also believed among the people that they are all expert in the field of archery. Their names were *Khoiri Linlang Sitpa, Phunan Telheiba, Mendi Ningthou Haotak Laiba* and *Chairel Ningthou.*[43] The religious idea behind this ritual is to pray them to protect the newly born child sfrom any type of evil spirit which might cause trouble to the child. Accordingly one of the maternal uncles of the child will shoot the arrow to the four directions and it will start from the direction of north east. The last arrow *i.e,* the fifth one will not shot. But it simply aims at the sky and below and it will keep inside the house until the newly born baby attains an age of three.[44] Then the whole process of ritual is completed after a robe made of black thread which is prepared for this purpose and tied around wrist of the baby.[45] Putting thread at the wrist of the child shows that the newly born child is properly protected from the evil eyes of any bad spirit.

In this long ritualistic process there is no room for any type of heavy expenditure from the members of the family side. Every ritual process is carried in a humble and simple way. There are no evidences about the involvement of the heavy expenditure from the family of the mother's side. It can be suggested that the idea of *Potyengba* which is a part of the duty of the family members of mother's side may be a new developmental phenomenon of the new religion. Still the people practice the morning ritual in the pattern of the traditional religion.

Death Ceremony

Like the birth of a new child the death of a person is also an important part of the life cycle of the human beings and its society. Therefore under the customary religion every society pays a great attention to the death of a person by performing several types of rites and rituals. The people begin to pay proper attention right from the time of the dying moment. That the people always take this particular moment as an important part of his or her life because this moment is considered the starting point of the last journey of the life of a particular person. This moment is highly sentimental and emotional part in the relationship between the person and their family in particular and society in general. It is the general believed among the people that just after the separation from the body the soul of the person would go direct to the place of the almighty God at the heaven. Therefore in order to have a peaceful last journey of the soul the people under their respective religious beliefs performe certain rites and rituals. This is generally called the death ceremony of a person.

Right from the earliest period of time the people of Manipur also performed the ceremony of the death of a person under their primordial religious concept and practices. The ritual is performed through several stages. As is done to other communities the people of this place also take the dying moment of a person as an important one. So, under this belief they always keep close vigil about the progress of the last moment of the life of the person. The moment the priest declares the death of the person the members of the family starts to arrange rituals. It is a long and systematic process. First the death body is kept inside a shed which is constructed with bamboo and thatch for the said purpose at the south eastern side of the courtyard. This shed is called *'Yathoksang'*. It is said that at a particular period of time the death body is kept inside the shed for five days.[46] But now this system is no longer continued. Then just after the completion of all the rites and rituals the coffin of the death body is taken to the cremation ground and disposed it with certain religious rites. This stage is known as *"Haoshi Mingthinba."*[47]

The disposal of dead body is followed by some religious practices which is made compulsory for the salvation of the departed soul. On the sixth days of the cremation the first religious ritual is performed by the members of the bereaved family. It is known as '*Leihun Tamba*'. On this very day the members of the family and friends offers flowers to the departed soul. It is performed on the cremation ground. After this on the twelve or thirteen days another ritual is performed called '*Lanna Thouram*'. It is also called' *Mathou Yangenba.*[48] Perhaps it may be related with the worshipping of Sun god. As already mentioned above, it affirms the significance of death as a part of the life of the people and society. Therefore in the case of the people of this place also they strictly follow the religious norms and practices for the welfare of the bereaved family and society in general. It is mentioned that on the tenth days from the day of the disposal of death body the priest (Maiba) cleans the house and members of the bereaved family. It was done just after the performing the rites of '*Atai Iratpa*''. [49] The cleaning of house by the priest is locally known as '*Yumsengba*' This is followed by the propitiation of *Pakhangba.*[50] another important diety. Then *Luwang Patcha Hanba and UshangAheiba* the priest would offer one cake of salt, one complete set of *cloth* and one cow to *Kasha*[51] a heavenly god. The basic purpose of this ritual is to make a positive way of the departed soul for going to the heavenly abode. And in order to get blessing from the Supreme god people would sing the verse of *Sanamahi Laihui, Pakhangba Laihui* and *Nongsaba Laihui.*[52] In this way the *Lanna thouram* or *Mathou Yangba* ceremony of the death person is completed.

Then it is followed by another ceremony called *Phiroy*. It is performed just after the completion of one year. It can be treated as the first death anniversary. But according to the ancient literary texts this first death anniversary is started from the period when the burial system of the disposal of death body is in practice. It is mentioned that immediately just after the completion of one year the death body would be taken out from the graveyard. Then after cleaning the skeleton and other parts only the head of the body was again buried with rites and rituals. This type of practice is called secondary burial system and it was in practice for quite long time. But just after the introduction of fire cremation system this practice is no longer continued and it is replaced by *Phiroy*.

It is also mentioned that this ceremony is performed with an objective to redeem all the debts which is to clear by the deceased person to his or her mother.[53] In this regard it is said that contribution of the mother so also of father to their children is beyond praiseworthy limit. The difficulties faced by the mother in the process of nurturing her children right from the moment of conceived stage until they attained certain age is something which is not forgettable by the children.[54] Therefore this ceremony is performed with feast to repay the debt. It is also known as *Amang Singkum* ceremony.[55] The feast is offered to the God and also dedicated to the parents of the deceased person. Along with this the ritual of *Atai Iratpa* and Kasha *Paotakpa* is also performed as it was done in the case of *Lanna Thouram*. After the completion of all ritualistic works the feast is offered to the elders and invitees. With this the ritual of Amang *Singkum* ceremony is completed. It is also a common belief among the people that if all the ritualistic process is performed in a defective way or not in a proper order the soul of the death body would not get deliverance.

Marriage (Luhongba or Haochong Kholoiba)

Like birth and death ceremony the marriage ceremony is also an equally important part in the life of the society. Apart from its relationship marriage also brings a spiritual relationship which renders a major contribution in the growth and development of the society. The concept of marriage is defined from various aspects. But in a simple understanding marriage is nothing but to establish a close relationship between man and women as husband and wife in order to have a family of their own in the system of the society. So every society performes certain ritualistic norms and patterns in the long process of marriage.

In Manipur the marriage is known as *Luhongba.* In the early period it was also called as *Haochong* kholoiba.[56] Many writers try to interpret this term in different ways. It is mentioned that the term *Luhongba* means to change the head. The word *Lu* means head and *hongba* means to change. It means that just after the marriage the woman change her identity from her parents to the side of her husband. It is also suggested that the term *Luhongba* might have been a derivated word from word *Nuhongba.*[57] The word *Nu* means penis and *hongba* means plenty. i.e. free availability of penis. This observation perhaps might be a hypothesis which cannot be treated as a scientific and appropriate interpretation. There are three systems through which the man and woman could establish the husband and wife relationship. First the system of 'engagement' between the parents of the two families, second the system of 'elopment' which is performed through the process of love relationship between man and woman and the third one is to take the woman forcibly by the man. These systems are known as 1. *Haina Singnaduna Luhongba* 2. *Chenba or Nupi chingba* and 3 *Chingba or Nupi Chingba.* Apart from the normal marriage system there are also two types of practices which are socially accepted as a kind of marriage. The names of this system are called *Keinya Katpa* and *Loukhatpa.*

Haina Singnaduna Luhongba (Marriage through engagement)

This type of marriage is performed through four ritualistic steps. The first step is *Hainaba* or *Nupi Haiba.* Under this system an emissary, may be a friend or a relative of the bridegroom's family have taken the initiative by going to the family of the bride with proposal for marriage. They go with some items like fruit and other sweetmeat. Generally such type of work is performed by the woman who is expert in this field. The second step is known as *Yathang Thaba* (to give formal order by the family of bride). In this process the agreement for marriage is confirmed by giving the formal order from the side of the bride's family. Here also some kind of religious rites is performed at the house of the girl. The third step is called *Waroipot Puba* (to carry the presentation for final agreement to the proposal of marriage. In this step people from the family side of the bridegroom will carry the items like cloth, fruits and other kinds of sweetmeat to the house of girl to mark of the beginning of the preparation for final stage of marriage. It is performed in a large scale in compared with the first two occasions. The offering of article to the deities is the main ritualistic ceremony of this function. Then it is followed by another step called *Heijing Kharai Puba or Heiton Kharai Pottamba.* This is the last step for the preparation of marriage. This ceremony is performed on an auspicious day fixed and agreed upon by both families. On this very day the people from the family side of the boy go in the form of procession by carrying all the requisite articles including the fruits to the house of the girl. The family of bride also invited friends and relatives just to receive the people coming from the side of the bridegroom. To worship god and goddesses *i.e.* ancestor of clan, local and guardian gods by offering articles arranged for this purpose is the main ritualistic part of the ceremony. After offering to the gods the fruits and other sweat meals are distributed to the peoples who attended the function.

Just after the completion of all these stages the marriage day is fixed on an auspicious day by both parents. Apart from others outward activities like the coming of bridegroom with friends, invitees and relatives the most important part is the performance of rites and rituals by offering article like fruits and sweets to the ancestor god and supreme god. The worship is done in a systematic way. First the supreme god is worshipped and then associated gods like *Koubru, Marjing, Wangbren, Thangjing.* etc. are also worshipped. After this *Imoinu Ahongbi*, the goddess of wealth is worshipped by offering a basket of rice with a salt plate, cotton, tobacco etc. and finally the selected women of the family of both sides set free Ngamu, a kind of small fish in the current water. This is also a part of rites and ritual of the marriage. Then after performing all these requisite ritualistic norms the mother of the bride as a mark of the beginning of marriage ties the rope specially arrange for this event on the palms of both bride and bridegroom. Thus after performing all the ritualistic parts of the marriage the bride is taken to the house of the in-laws. Before entering inside house she is welcomed by the members of the in-laws family with torch in their hand and by throwing *Kabok Aphanba*, a kind of parched rice to the bride. Then she is taken inside the house by her mother-in-law. Then just after giving salutation to the household deity god *Sanamahi* and *Leimarel Sidabi* the bride is taken to the room specially allotted to her. With this long process the marriage ceremony of the pattern of first category is completed.

Chenba (Elopement)

The second category of marriage is performed just after the elopement. In this case some of the steps which is performed in the first category is not practice. Since the elopement is done after having a mutual agreement between male and female the question of sending feelers by the family of bridegroom to the house of bride with the proposal for marriage is no longer required. Therefore to get formal approval which is performed in the first category i.e. *Yathang Thaba* function is also not practiced. Except these two the remaining steps are of the same nature. But there is also another exception in the case of second category of marriage. If there is no agreement for marriage between the two families, sometimes the marriage is performed at the house of the bridegroom's family. In such cases all the steps of a regular marriage system is shortened. But the problem lies on the bride. That if the ritualistic functions are not done the bride is excommunicated by her parents. Even in some extremely orthodox family, the in-laws refuse to take any type of food prepared and cooked by her. Such cases are solved by another marriage system called *Loukhatpa*. It is a very simple form of betrothal. It is compulsory for those women who marry in the house of their husband without the participation of her family. In a simple sense *Loukhatpa* means to remove the burden of excommunication of their daughter or sister by members of her family. To worship the ancestor gods, local deities and supreme god by offering fruits and other items brought from the family of the bridegroom is the main function of the ceremony. It is always performed at the house of the bride.

Keinya Katpa (to offer bride)

Another system of marriage is known *as Keinya Katpa.* 'Keinya' means bride and 'Katpa' means to offer. It means to offer the bride. It is the most simple and less expensive system of marriage. It is also said that such type of marriage is a commonly practiced among the people of rural areas and poor people.[59] But this observation may not be considered as true because right from time immemorial people get married through normal ritualistic pattern. Such type of marriage is performed only in some exceptional cases in order to get recognition from the society. It is a known fact that in the society of Manipur there is no restriction to the remarriage of widow or divorcee. In such cases marriage is performed either through *Loukhatpa* or *Keinya katpa* system. Only the ritualist part of the Keinya Katpa system is to prepare a pair of garland. After offering to god Sanamahi first the women will put the garland on the neck of the male and in the same the male again returns it. This ceremony is performed at the presence of elderly people of both families. The other items which are brought from the family of groom's side will be offered to other deities like ancestor god and guardian god. The ceremony comes to an end after taking feast arranged by the family of bride.

This type of betrothal is practiced in the case of adultery also. If the culprits are caught while they are indulging in their wrongful activities they are made husband and wife forcibly by the people through *Keinya Katpa* system. The people also force the male who commit adultery to pay bride price (*Nupi Mamal*). There is no ritualistic work in such cases.

Festivals

Apart from these cyclystic ritualistic ceremonies the people also enjoy various types of festivals which are more or less closely related with traditional religious concept. Some of the important festivals are *Chinggoi Irruppa, Cheiraoba, Heikru Hidongba, Mera Haochongba Ningol Chakkouba* etc.

1. Chinggoi Irruppa

It is a very popular festival which is closely connected with the belief of the traditional religion. *Chinggoi* is a name of a small hill river flowing in the *Nongmaiching Ching*, a name of a mountain in the state. The name *Chinggoi Irruppa* means to take bath at the *Chinggoi River*. After the adoption of Hindu religion as the state religion it is known as *Chinggoi Baruni* or *Baruni khurumba* means to give salutation to *Baruni*. It is celebrated every year on a particular day which falls three days before the new moon. On this day the people of both male and female irrespective of ages go in group to this particular hill to worship the deities which are located at different places in natural way. Generally the people belief this hill as an important place as it is closely connected with the mythical history which is related with the cosmology according to the traditional religion. However before going to other deities the worshippers cleans their bodies by taking bath in the *Chinggoi* River. In this process the people offer flowers, small quantity of rice and other articles which the people desired to offer to god. After taking bath the people then move to the places of other deities. From this practice the *Chinggoi Iruppa* festival is considered as one of the greatest religious festival of the state.

2. Cheiraoba

It is also another important religious festival which is closely connected with the cultural life of the people of Manipur. This festival is celebrated on the first day of the month of *Sajibu* (March/April) and it marks the beginning of new year. From this particular idea it is also known as *Sachifu Lakyen Taiba.*[60] To offer articles like cloth,fruits,flowers,vegetables to the household deities like *Sanamahi and Leimarel* is the main function of the festival. Then as a mark of enjoying the coming of *New Year* every houses prepares a special meal and it is also offered to the house hold deities and other deities of surrounding areas. For the deities of surrounding areas the items of meal is placed at the main gate of the house. On this day every people put new cloth and to give some portion of the cook item to the house of relatives and friends is also a very important part of the festival. Then after taking meal the people of irrespective of ages climbed the nearby hill to worship gods. Thus the people enjoy this religious festival in a most colourful way.

3. Heikru Hitongba

It is also another type of religious festival enjoyed by the people as an important part of the cultural life of the state. It is a kind of boat race performed only after offering the garland of *Heikru, (Emblic myrobalam* or *Phylanthus emblic* in Botanical term), a kind of fruit to the god. From this pattern it is popularly known as *Heikru Hitongba.* This festival is held every year on the eleventh day of the month *Langban*(August/September). It is performed at a moat which is situated near the temple of *Bijoy Govinda* a deity of Hindu religion. As a part of the ritualistic of this festival every sailors including the leader called *Tengmai Leppa* will put the garland of *Heikru* on their neck. It is said that this garland is prepared with a specific style for this festival. Accordingly a kind of herb called *Hup* is put between two fruit and the number of Heikru should be fixed at 108(one hundred and eight). Another type of garland of rice with a specific number of 108(one hundred and eight) is also prepared to offer to the god[61].

4. Mera Haochongba

This is also another important festival which is celebrated for quite long time as a mark of remembrance of the national solidarity among the different ethnic group of people in the state and to give more strength in the process of the further consolidation of the idea of Manipuri nationalism. It is a historical fact that the population of Manipur is constituted on the basic foundation of pluralism. From the ground reality it can be suggested that right from the ancient time some kind of autonomy is enjoyed by every ethnic people in their own way and it is also accepted by the central authority *i.e.* the king of the state. However, in spite of all these political structure people has full loyalty to the supreme authoritityship of the king. Therefore to show their loyalty to the king and to mark oneness to the growth of nationalism in the state this festival is observed in a large scale way. This is performed every year in the month of Mera(September/

October) in which all the village chiefs and peoples of respective villages from the surrounding hill areas fully participate. The presentation of gifts of any kind available in their villages to the king and performance of cultural show and sports are the main function of this day. In return of this the king also presents cloths and other articles to the village chiefs and peoples. Indeed it is a big festival so a large scale arrangement is made under the direct supervision of the king and accommodation and feast is also prepared by him. The entire responsibility is put to a department called *Hao Macha Loisang* (Office of tribal Affaires). Thus through this festival the king of Manipur is able to maintain the harmonious relationship among the people of the state and at the same time it also strengthens the spirit of national character among the people.

5. Ningngol Chakkouba

It is also another one of the greatest and colourful festival in which all the people of the state irrespective of rich and poor are actively involved. It is a long tradition and it is even said that this festival is performed from the time of the period of deities.[62] The main objective of the festival is to invite the daughters and sisters by the fathers or brothers to take meal specially prepared for the purpose. In a way this day is a special day for married daughters and sisters irrespective of ages. It is mentioned that this practice is a continuation from the time of *Nongda Lairen Pakhangba* the first historical king of Manipur i.e. in 33 A.D. The festival is originated from a very interesting background. It is recorded that *Laisna*, the queen of *Pakhangba*, one day went to the harvesting place of her elder brother *Poireiton* just to see the progress of the work. He was very happy to see his sister after a long time and a marked of sister and brother love relationship *Poireiton* gave her two types rice, i.e. black rice and white rice along with a bunch of banana. She was very pleased to see the affectionate attitude of her brother and so she invited him for a lunch to her place.[63] Thus from that afterwards, and as mark of remembrance the married sisters invited their brothers every year on a particular day. But that practice is changed from the time of King Chandrakirti Singh (1850-1886). From the time of his reigning period the married sisters and daughters are invited by the father or brother to their house. Apart from the special feast arranged for them the presentation of gifts is also another aspect of this festival.

From these above evidences it is quite clear that right from the very ancient time Manipur has enjoyed a fantastic traditional religious concept and ideas. Through this foundation the people also enjoy various types of religious festivals which give a lot of help in the process of the strengthening and fostering the distinctive cultural and religious identity of the state and people.

REFERENCES

1. *Oxford Dictionary.*
2. Gangmumei Kamei, *Essays on Primordial Religion,* 2006, p.9.
3. William P. Scott, *Dictionary of Socialism,* 1999, p.344.
4. E.B. Tylor, *Dictionary of Anthropology,* Pub.1990, p.451.
5. *Ibid.*
6. Christopher Partridge(ed) *The World's Religion,* p.13.
7. Marx and Engel, *On Religion,* Revised Edition 1988, p.128.
8. *Dictionary of Philosophy*, Progress Publication, p.357.
9. Christopher Partridge(ed), *op. cit.*, p.13.
10. *The Encyclopedia of Philosophy,* p. 143.
11. *Ibid.,* p.144.
12. *Ibid.,* p. 143.
13. *Ibid.*
14. *Ibid.*, p.144.
15. *Ibid.*
16. Frank Byron Jevon, *History of Religion,* p. 2.
17. Gangmumei Kamei, *op. cit.,* p.9.
18. Collins Hohu, *Anthropology, Culture, Society and Evolution*, Pub.1975, p. 417.
19. *Ibid.*
20. Gangmumei Kamei, *op. cit.,* p.15.
21. *Ibid.*

22. Christopher Partridge(ed) *op. cit.,* p. 101.
23. Gangmumei Kamei, *op. cit.,* pp.13-14.
24. *Ibid.,* p.15.
25. Christopher Partridge(ed), *op. cit.,* p.102.
26. *Ibid.,* p.132.
27. K.C. Tensuba, *Meitrabak (Encyclopedia)*(Manipuri), 2008, p. 558.
28. Dr. Bheigya Yengkhoiba, *Leithak Leikharol*, 1994, p. 2.
29. Sairem Nilbir, *Laiyingthou Sanamahi Amasung Sanamahi Laining Hingat Ihou* (Manipuri), 2002, p. 1.
30. M. Gourachandra, *Sanamahi Laihui* (Manipuri), p.1.
31. *Ibid.,* p. 2.
32. *Ibid.,* p. 3.
33. E.B. Taylor, *op. cit.,* p.142.
34. Christopher Partridge(ed), *op. cit.,* p.407.
35. *Ibid.*
36. William P. Scott, *op. cit.,* p. 11.
37. Frank Byron Jevon, *op. cit.,* p. 89.
38. *Encyclopedia of Religion and Ethics,* Vol.1, p. 535.
39. *The New Encyclopedia Britanica,* Vol.1 p. 421.
40. *Encyclopedia of Religion and Ethics,* Vol.1 p. 535.
41. Christopher Partridge (ed), *op. cit.* p. 214.
42. Dr. N. Birchandra Singh, *The Meitei Society, A Study on Traditional Life Circle Ceremony,* 2006, p. 28.
43. *Ibid.*
44. *Ibid.*
45. *Ibid.*
46. *Ibid.,* p. 109.
47. Pombilon, Quoted by Birchandra, p. 126.
48. *Ariba Manipuri Longei* (Manipuri), p. 227.
49. Thongam Madhop Singh. *Khunung Lichat Sajat* (Manipuri), 2006, Second Shri N. Khelchandra Singh Edition, p.77.
50. Sakok Lamlel (Manipuri), p.8.

51. The name 'Kasa' is used in two terms. One is the 'Soraren' the king of heaven and another is 'Unclean God'.
52. Khunung Lichat Sajat, p.78.
53. N. Birachandra Singh, *op. cit.*, p.127.
54. *Ibid.*, p.128.
55. *Ibid.*
56. Ariba Manipuri Longei (Manipuri), State Kala Academy, Manipur, p. 224.
57. N. Birchandra *op. cit.*, p.53.
58. Khunung Lichat Sajat (Manipuri), p.76.
59. N.Birchandra, *op. cit.*, p.59.
60. Khulem Chandrasekhar, *Inatki Harao Kummei*, (Manipuri), p.39.
61. *Ibid.*, p.85.
62. *Ibid*., p.114.
63. *Ibid.*, p.115.

3

Hindu Colonialism

The process of Hindu prosetelyzing activities and religious colonialism in Manipur was started with the gradual penetration of Brahmin missionary activists from the other areas of mainland India. The archival sources evidenced that the activities of Hindu religious missionary began to enter in Manipur from the early period of time. Gangmumei said that "Manipur had already came into contact with Hinduism in the form of worship of Vishnu since the middle of fifteen century"[1]. However large scale migration of different groups of people from mainland India and their colonization process with Indo-Chinese peninsular and East Indies are to be studied it can be suggested that the missionary zeal of the Brahmans and Buddhists,[2] apart from the interest of commercial enterprise, was also one of the noteworthy factor for the increase of their population in these areas. Regarding the activities of the Buddhist missionary activities in Manipur, it is mentioned that in order to propagate their religious principles and ideas some Buddhist elements reached China by crossing the plain and hill areas of Manipur[3]. However, the complete absence of any traces of Buddhism has created a serious problem in the process of the establishment of the nature of the presence of Buddhist elements in the country. In early period of time the people of India used three different routes for going to China. The road from Pataliputra (modern Patna) through Assam and Upper Burma near

Bhamo and proceeded over the mountains and across the river valley to Ynanfu (Kunming) the main city of the southern province of China was also one of the three routes.[4] At that time, according to ancient texts, there were a regular trade relationship between China and Manipur particularly in silk trade industry. And people used this route for many purposes. It is mentioned that Buddhist missionary reached China from Mauryan India[5]. According to Li Tai San Pao Chi (The Record Concerning the Three Treasures Under Successive Dynasties) which was written at the end of six century, a group of eighteen Buddhist monks headed by Shih-Li-Fang, by carrying a number of Buddhist scripts, reached the Chinese court in the 3rd century B.C.[6] According to S. Sasanananda "the Buddhism spread in Asian by the efforts of Asokan Buddhist missionaries who went to South East Asian countries, particularly Suvana Bhumi by the land route through Assam". On the basis of this information he was of the opinion that Buddhism was introduced into this region during the period i.e. in the 3rd century B.C.[7] Though the information was not fully substantiated, it shows that at a particular stage of the early period of time there were a steady flow of intercourse between the Buddhist monks and people of China and Burma by using this land route. In this connection it is also mentioned that about 300 B.C. one Khaba Toren Kha, the king of Manipur made an attempt to make Buddhism as the state religion. But since the common people was against it the missionary people of Budhism left for China.[8] But the authenticity of this information is not fully established and verified. Therefore it can be left as a subject for further research. The Chinese believed that Buddhists entered China during the reign of Mingti (58-75). On the other hand, it is also said that people heard of the activities of Buddhist monks in China before this time.[9] Whatever the case may be but from these evidences it can be suggested that there might have been some activities of Buddhism in Manipur in the Pre-Nongda Lairen Pakhangba period.

One of the basic nature and character of the Hindu colonization process, as pointed out by R.C. Majumdar was that the emigrants permanently settled in foreign lands, married the local women and try to influence their superior culture and gradually Hinduised the society.[10] Such type of gradual penetration was further aided by the active missionary propaganda and their efforts to spread religious influence in the art, culture, idea and social life of the country. The local people assumed names and adopted Sanskrit language, religion, manner and customs. At the same time the emigrants imbibed local habits and social usages and merged themselves into the local communities.[11] Thus, it greatly helped in the process of Hindu colonialistic practices and it created a situation of a flood gate for the coming of fresh streams of immigrants from the areas outside the country.

The first wave of immigration of 'Brahmins' was started from the period of King Kyamba (1467-1508 A.D.) i.e. 15th century. During his reigning period eighteen[12] Brahmins from the different parts of India entered into Manipur. They were permitted to settle in the state and allowed them to marry the local girls. Accordingly new family names were given to them. And thus they became Manipuris. But it is also mentioned that Brahmins began to enter even before Kyamba.[13] But there was no substantial evidence to support this claim. After this a series of Brahmins had entered into Manipur and this trend was continued the Hinduism was fully flourished in this country. According to the record the Brahmins continued to enter into Manipur even during the period of King Churachand Singh (1891-1941 A.D.). During his period four Brahmins had entered into Manipur and they made their settlement in the country, married the local women. Then after getting new family name they were allowed to settle in Manipur.[14] Thus, as mentioned in the local literary texts seventy-nine Brahmins entered into Manipur and they married the local girls and they established the Brahmin family in the state. Along with this they also took a great initiative role in the process for the spread of the ideas of Hinduism in the state.

The history of the development of Hindu religious influence in Manipur may be classified into four sections. First, contact with Hinduism in the form of worship through Vishnu in the middle of fifteen century. Second, growth of Ramandi Cult in the eighteenth century. Third, the introduction of Vaishnava Cult during the period of Bheigyachandra. Fourth, the rise of the despotic religious authoritative power of Brahman Samaj in nineteenth and twentieth century.

Beginning of Vishnu Worship

It has already been mentioned above about the coming of Brahmins in Manipur during the reign of King Kyamba. From this point of view his period may be treated as an important landmark in the history of the development of Hinduism in this state. Another significant aspect of his period was the beginning of the influence of the Hinduism through the form of worshipping of Vishnu. The historical background of the connection of Hinduism with the people of Manipur was a unique and noteworthy feature. It is recorded that King Thangwai Ningthouba, later on he was known as Kyamba, (1467-1508 A.D.), made a joint expedition with King Choupha Khe Khomba of Pong, against the king of Kyang or Kyaang Khambaat[15] a Shan kingdom in the Kabaw Valley area. The combined expedition force defeated the Kyang and victory celebration was organized with great pomp. The nature of the celebration was distinctively mentioned in the royal chronicle of Manipur. And it also mentioned that after this victory the name Thangwai Ningthouba was changed to 'Kyamba' the conqueror of Kyang. As a mark of mutual friendship the two kings exchanged their servants. The king of Pong gave his mouth organ player to the king of Manipur and in return king Kyamba gave two dream drummers to the king of Pong and they also fixed a common boundary line between two the countries. These are all properly mentioned in the official record.

Another aspect of the friendship relationship between the king of Manipur and Pong was the presentation of the statue of Lord Vishnu. It is mentioned that just after the end of the expedition king Choupha Khe Khomba presented a stone image of a God (Pha) which riding over Garuda.[16] Besides this the king of Pong also presented a golden casket of the value of 80 (eighty) mohar of gold.[17] Different versions were advanced by writers particularly about the background of the presentation of Vishnu. L. Ibungohal Singh claimed that the "Vishnu image had been in Manipur as a family God of the ruling prince from the pre-historic days".[18] He further said that this image was taken by the king of Pong as the war trophy when he conquered Manipur. As a mark of insult to the people of Manipur the king of Pong used the image as an instrument for scratching the itches. But the itches became ulcer. So, when the friendship was established he returned it to Kyamba. Another story is that the symbol of Vishnu fell down like a bull of fire from the sky.[19] King Khe Khomba of Pong used it as an instrument for scratching itches, which became ulcer. The king did not know the identity of the image. Then it was revealed in his dream that the statue was of a God. Therefore after the end of the joint campaign he gave the statue to Kyamba. But, one of the biggest confusing parts behind all these informations is the lack of supporting evidences. Whenever there were any questions of authenticity of any historical event and information, the writers and scholars always referred to the two great texts i.e. Cheitharol Kumbaba and Ningthourol Lambuba.

Compared with other royal chronicles of neighbouring countries the *Cheitharol Kumbaba* of Manipur may be regarded as the most scientific and well-informed sources of the history of this country. It keeps records of every events and occasion whether it may be minor or major. Even the nature of the establishment of friendship relationship between Kyamba and the king of Pong was clearly well recorded in the *Cheitharol Kumbaba*. Apart from this the nature of the exchange of people of different profession was also entered in this royal chronicles. Surprisingly such an important event i.e. the presentation of Vishnu statue, which creates a watershed for the future history of Manipur is not reflected in the royal chronicles. In addition to this there is also another royal text i.e. *'Ningthourol Lambuba,* which mainly dealt with the activities of the king, queens and other members of the royal family. In this royal text also nothing was mentioned about the nature of the presentation of Vishnu statue. The only information mentioned in the *Cheitharol Kumbaba* is that it was the gem of Khe Khomba King of Pong, which he weared as necklace around his neck. This gem was placed in front of Kyamba and king of Pong when they were sitting together at court (Kuchu). From this it can be suggested that it was not the statue of Vishnu but the gem of the king of Pong.[21] The absence of information about a very important event in these two important royal texts may lay a foundation for a big debate particularly on the question of the authenticity of this information. The question is whether the issue of the presentation of Vishnu statue was an act of the art of interpolations which was developed just after the full flourishment of Hinduism in Manipur.

It is also mentioned that king Kyamba directed his officials to find out a Brahmin who would be able to worship the Vishnu. The royal servants found some Brahmins taking bath at Paonam Hiden at the bank of Imphal River inside the present Kangla Fort. They brought them to the king. They identified it as the statue of Vishnu. Then the king entrusted the responsibilities of the worship of Vishnu to one Bhanu Narayan[21] who had been sheltering in a Manipuri house at Lairikyengbam Leikai. Later on his descendents were known as Phurailatpam. But the ancient text mentioned that one Subhi Narayan[22] came to Manipur from Western Takhel (Tripura) and married Thoinu a lady of Haokei group. His surname was known as Phurailatpam. As already mentioned above about the coming of eighteenth Brahmins in Manipur during the period of Kyamba. They were 1) Phurailatpam, 2) Pitambar Cheithaba Mayum, 3) Pandamayum, 4) Shrimayum, 5) Gotimayum, 6) Sijagurumayum, 7) Kakchingtabam, 8) Adhikarimayum, 9) Sitrammayum, 10) Baspatimayum, 11) Leikhunchangbam Mayum, 12) Sanjukimayum, 13) Dhyandas Mayum, 14) Takhelchangbam Mayum, 15) Leihaothabam.[23] Out of these eighteen, one Brahmin who came from Nadia did not establish his family and other two persons coming from Kanpur and Sylhet along with their family had entered into the line of Leihaothabam and Kakchingtabam,[24] respectively.Therefore they are not included in the lists. It is also observed that the coming of Brahmins along with the knowledge of Sanskrit script and astrology had enriched the cultural life of the.[25]

It is also mentioned that king Kyamba had constructed a Vishnu temple by brick at Bishenpur.[26] It is also said that Vishnu temple was constructed by the artisans coming from Bengal and settled at Lammangdong. But according to the available records of the ancient texts, the art of the making of brick was learned by the Manipuri people from the Khagi (Chinese) during the period of king Khagemba. If this information is taken as an authentic or near authentic then the issue of the construction of Vishnu temple by brick has put at a big question because king Khagemba ruled in the later period. From this fact it can be suggested that the temple might be constructed either by indigenous materials like, wood and bamboo. But the claim of the construction of Vishnu temple by brick is to be analysed from the basis of the accepted available records, it can be observed that the informations perhaps may be an art of interpolation which was developed in later period in order to strengthen the concept of Hinduism in the minds of the people of the country. It was claimed that the temple was constructed by a Bengali masonry. But the architectural style shows that it was constructed by a person who was conversant with the Pagoda architecture of Bengal.[27] It is said that according to India Silpa text only three styles were recognized. They are the Nagara style, the Vabera style and Dravida style. But the present temple of Bishnupur cannot be put either of the two categories.[28] Since the importance of the influence of Hinduism was not there at that particular period of time the worship of Vishnu was started in an innocuous way.[29] But in later period when the influence of Hinduism was fully in operational stage, the image of Vishnu was kept in the temple of Govindajee.[30]

From the above facts it can be suggested that though the worship of Vishnu was initiated at the royal patronage there was no evidence to show that king Kymba was converted to Hinduism. At that time he was a strong believer of traditional religious practices. Even the migration of Brahmins did not make any change in the religion and social equilibrium of his period. Rather they were absorbed into the social fabric of the Meitei community after getting clan name and through intermarriage with local women. However, the beginning of the practice of the worshipping Vishnu and Hindu deity is a very important beginning for the establishment of Hindu colonialism in Manipur. This particular event gave a small beginning for the increase of the importance of Brahmin group in the social hierarchy of the state. Although the king was not converted to Hinduism the action of the ruler clearly indicates the inclination of royal patronage to the free movements of the Brahmin from outside Manipur. Such type of development gave a good opportunity to open a floodgate for the migration of Brahmin in a large-scale way in later periods. This was happened exactly in the subsequent periods. Therefore the introduction of Vishnu worship during the period of king Kyamba may be treated as a beginning of Hindu colonialism in Manipur.

Growth of Ramandi Cult

The second phase of the activities of Hindu colonialism in Manipur was started in full scale during the period of king Garibniwaz (Pamheiba, 1709-1749 A.D.). He was one of the greatest kings of Ningthouja dynasty. During his period Manipur attained the zenith of her glory in every aspects of the life of the country. Prof. Gangmumei said, "Yet no king in Manipur's history was so controversial than Garibniwaz, perhaps due to the highly embittered religious controversies of his times in which he was personally involved and resultant persistent efforts of his religious detractor to malign him."[31] T.C. Hodson wrote, "To the royal will Pamheiba, the monarch in whose reign the fortunes of the state reached their zenith, Hinduism owes its present position as the official religion of the state"[32]. It has already been mentioned about the inclination royal patronage to the Brahmin immigrants. This environment was a great opportunity to the Brahmins who desired to enter into Manipur. Therefore, the regular flow of Brahmins was continued till the reign of Garibniwaz the number of Brahmins who entered into Manipur and made their settlement with the family was reached to sixty-four.[33] Even during the period of Garibniwaz 10 (Ten) Brahmins entered into Manipur and out of these total numbers 9 (Nine) Brahmins made their settlement and married the local women. It is also mentioned that one Brahmin monk Santidas from Sylhet married the daughter of

Pamheiba (Garibniwaz). But they had no issue.[34] It has already been already mentioned above that though king Kyamba showed royal patronage to the Brahmin immigrants there were no evidence and sign of the Hinduism in the religious practices in Manipur. Even the continuity of the practice of the worship of Vishnu was not properly recorded in the subsequent period of time. During the period of king Khagemba (1597-1652 A.D.) the traditional religious practices were fully flourished. But during the period of king Charairongba (1697-1709 A.D.) there was a sign of Hindu religious influence in the life of the people of the state. During his reigning period eighteen Brahmins entered into Manipur and after getting married with local women they settled here with a family name. Out of these total numbers of persons, some had entered into the family, which had already existed. The name of the families were 1) Laipubam, 2) Hangoibam, 3) Monohormayum, 4)Gopal Hanjaba Mayum, 5) Guru Aribam Mayum, 6) Laimayum, 7) Choudhurimayum, and 8) Guru Aribam.[35] He himself was formally initiated to Hinduism in the year 1704 A.D.[36] It is said that king Charairongba was initiated to Vaishnavism by one Krishnacharya alias Rai Vanamali from Shweta Ganga, Puri[37] in the month of Sajibu (April-May). Since he was the guru of the king his descendents were known later on as Guru Aribam. However, it is a strange to note that the person called Krishnacharya was not figured in the Bamon Khunthoklon (Migration of Brahmins) which is considered as the most authentic sources of the history in migration of Brahmins in Manipur. It is simply mentioned that one Brindaban Brahmin came from Orissa and his family was known as Guru Aribam.[38] Whatever may be but during the reign of Charairongba, though converted to Vaishnavism, he did not totally break off from traditional religion.

The construction of the temple of Krishna was one of the most notable contributions of king Charairongba. It was followed by the construction of temple of Kali or Kalika.[39] On the other hand; he also constructed the temple of Laiwahaiba (Sanamahi). From these evidences it can be observed that though Charairongba formally converted to Hinduism he never made any attempt to impose the

Hindu religious practices to the people. Rather he gave an equal treatment to both religious practices. But from the history of the religious development point of view it can be observed that the period of king Charairongba was very significant that his conversion to Hinduism and his great patronizing attitude to the new religion had produced a great positive impact for the consolidation of Hindu colonialism activities in the country. This was clearly evidenced by the later religious developments.

The reign of king Garibniwaz (Pamheiba – 1709-1748 A.D.) was the most important period for two reasons. First his religious policy had produced a death-blow to the traditional religious practices and secondly, it laid the basic foundation for a complete transformation of the social life of the people under the influence of the Hindu way of life. In regard to the nature of the religious policy of Pamheiba; T.C. Hodson observed that "at first the decrees of the king received but little obedience, and the opposition to the change centered mainly around the numerous members of the royal family who were supported, not unnaturally, by the Maibas, the priests of the older religion. Religious dissent was treated with the same ruthless severity as was meted out to political opponents and wholesale banishment and execution drove the people into acceptance of the tenants of Hinduism."[40] To make Hinduism as the state religion, King Pamheiba had this new religious practice. So in order to materialize his desire he made a series of successful attempt to impose the idea of new religion upon the people and punishment was given to those individuals and groups who refused to accept it. Apart from this he also made an attempt to destroy all the important areas and sites of traditional religion and replaced it by Hindu names.

It seems that at the beginning Pamheiba was also a lover and patron of the traditional religious practices. As mark of respect to the traditional religion he created a stone sculpture of Laiwahaiba (Sanamahi) at Leishangkhong and in the month of Kalen (May and June) he also constructed a pond of Laiwahaiba at Leishangkhong.[41] During his reigning period 10 (Ten) Brahmins entered into Manipur and they were allowed to settle and marry the local girls. Out of these, six Brahmins got their separate family names and remaining four entered into the line of other family line. The six families were 1) Hanjaba Mayum, 2) Sanjuki Mayum, 3) Tikhakmayum, 4) Hajarimayum, 5) Hidangmayum, 6) Anouba,[42] etc. It is also recorded that during his reigning period 39 (Thirty-nine) Bairagis from outside including the guru of Ahom king arrived at Manipur.[43] But the royal chronicle did not mention anything about Gopal Das under whose guidance Garibaniwaz was initiated to Vaishnavism in the year 1717. It is believed that Guru Gopal Das might be one of the members of the Bairagis. However, a number of questions may be raised about the real identity of the religious cult under the framework of Vaishnavism. It is mentioned that Charairongba accepted Nimandi or Nimbarka School of Vaishnavism i.e. the worship of Radha Krishna image. On the other hand he also encouraged the religious concept of 'Saktaism' by constructing the temple of 'Kalika'.[44] The same practice was also going on during the period of Garibniwaz. He also constructed the temple of 'Kalika'. From these evidences it can be presumed that the religious concept of 'Saktaism' might be practiced in Manipur even before the coming of Ramandi Cult.

The arrival of Santi Das Gosai as a religious preacher at Manipur was a great landmark in the whole process of religious and social life of the country. It is said that king Garibniwaz followed Vaishnavism for about 20(twenty) years.[45] During this period, Manipur made a successful attempt to popularise this religious concept among the people along with 'Bhagavat'[46] a sacred religious book of Hinduism.' Thus,Vaishnavism became the state religion. However, this information was not corroborated with other evidences. It is true that the king accepted Hinduism but he did not make any attempt to establish the Hindu religion as state religion. On the other side he did not ignore the traditional religious practices. The whole religious transformation was developed only after the coming of Santi Das. It is mentioned that Santi Das was forced by the God of traditional religion to go to Manipur[47] and preached the Hindu religious concept.[48] Indeed, it was a very interesting myth created perhaps, in the later period to justify his action. Thus this type of myth was interpreted by some people in such a way that he was forced by the traditional supreme God of this place to preach his religious idea in Manipur. Indeed it is a very interesting myth created by the people and scholars of that period of time to justify the arrival of Santi Das and his religious missionary activities. Thus the propagation of a new religion was actively started after 1720 with the full support of the king. He advised the king to issue royal diction for the introduction of many changes in the religious and social practices of the people.

Still the people are not able to ascertain on the question of how and when the name of this place had changed from traditional to the present Sanskrit name. It is believed that the present name might have been emerged after conversion to Hinduism. As mentioned in Sanamahi Laikan the present name was changed during period of Garibniwaz[49]. But the information about the change of name of the country is not properly recorded in the *Cheitharol Kumbaba*. The absence of information about this important issue in the royal chronicle has created certain confusion among the researchers on the question of why it was not reflected in the official record. And why was this issue mentioned only in the Sanamahi Laikan? Whatever it may be but as a part of his missionary activities he introduced a series of changes in the social and religious practices of the people. The rearing of pig and keeping of poultry were banned in urban area.[50] The eating of meat by the people was declared as forbidden. Those who reared pig and poultry were sent to the countryside or far places. The temples of nine 'Umanglais'[51] were completely destroyed. By a royal decree the responsibility of the worship of royal deities like 'Nongsaba', 'Yumthei Lai', 'Panthoibi', 'Taibang Khaiba' (Sanamahi) was given to the Brahmins[52].The opening of burial places of former kings, queens, princess was also another religious action of Santi Das., which was a sacrilege for the Meiteis according to their religious customs. On 20th Lamdas of 1725 (Sunday) the king opened burial grounds of these royal personalities and the skeletons were exhumed and cremated again on fire. Then the ashes were immerged in the Chinduin River.[53] From these facts it can be observed that cremation on fire was not in practice and it was introduced only from the time of Garibniwaz. It is also mentioned that this new practices was introduced at the dictation of Mussalman guru. These changes brought a drastic impact in the social and religious life of the people. This system also introduced by king at his dictation.[54]

To put sacred books and other literary woks on fire was undoubtedly an unfortunate action of the king and Santi Das. This event is still popularly known as 'Puya Meithaba' (the burning of Puyas). The royal chronicle did not give any type of detail picture about the nature of the event. Simply it mentioned about the burning of books on 17th Sunday of the month of Mera.[55] It is said that the reference to the burning of books was made by one Khumanthem Kaomacha in his book, '*Manipuri Ittibriti* (1934)' in which he mentioned a list of 123 books.[56] Shri Atombapu Sharma in his book, "Pakhangba' gave a critical observation about the religious policy of Santi Das. He said that this monk, with an objective to root out the entire religious practices had burnt down all the ancient books.[57] Whatever the case may be, such type of action may be treated as an attempt to demolish completely the distinctive identity of the people of this country. This action was rightly observed as an unethical action on the part of the king at his preceptor.[58] It is said that one Lourembam Khongnangthaba who was a great Scholar Philosopher of the period of Garibniwaz put a strong protest against the introduction of new changes which was not at all on the line of the desire of the masses. But royal chronicle did not make any type of references about his effort.

The destruction of the abodes of traditional deities was also another significant feature of the king and his preceptor. As a part of their programme the king destroyed the images of 'Umanglais' and other important deities like Layingthou, Panthoibi, Laiwahaiba, Soraren, Hoidonpokpi, etc. This action was known among the people as 'Sanamahi' Kolu Yeikhaiba' (Destruction of the image of Sanamahi). The images of these deities were buried at Mongbahanba, (now popularly known as Mahaballi). On the other hand, as a mark to promote and foster the new religion the king constructed the temple of *Krishna* and *Kalika* near the big tank at Wangkhei Leikai. Along with this the chronicle also mentioned about the burning of the houses of royal family. Some scholars tried to interpret it as a mark of expression of resentment among the people to the policy of the king and his preceptor.[59] Then in order to destroy the religious identity of Mongbahanba the king established the stone image of Hanuman, a legendary monkey hero of *Ramayana* at this place. The name of this place was also changed from Mongbahanba to Mahaballi forest. The image of Hanuman was made from the stone slab which was erected at the centre of the market place.[60] The temple of Hanuman was inaugurated on 11th Wednesday of the month of *Hiyangei* (October and November).[61] It is also said that Santi Das carried out his continued efforts to destroy the importance of the abode of traditional religion. Thus with help of these actions he tried to consolidate the influence of the Ramandi Cult. While this was the situation Shanti Das had come across some kind of unnatural accidents which forced him to stop all kinds of his action for a successful religious colonizing process. It is also mentioned that while he made an attempt to destroy the abode of Goddess *Heibokching*, the deity itself came out in the form of human body and tried to kill him. He was very much afraid to see such type of unnatural powers of the local deities. Then, he immediately stopped his entire attempt to destroy the abode of important deities and suggested the king to protect and preserve these religious sacred Thus just after realizing the power and importance of the local deities particularly the goddess, he immediately identified them as the symbol of power(*Shakti*) and addressed them as '*Devi*' under the Hindu religious concept. Then at his suggestion the king again constructed the temple and image of Laiwa Haiba (Sanamahi) in 1729 and in 1733 the temple of Sanamahi, which was destroyed earlier was also restored. This was not the end of his effort to establish the religious colonialism in Manipur. As a first step he asked the king and his close relatives to wear a religious thread on their body. It is recorded that on the full moon day of Wakching (December and January) the king and Santi Das took a bath at the confluence of Imphal and Iril River at Lillong to the southern side of Imphal city and put sacred religious thread on the body of the king.[62] This particular event may be marked as the beginning of the consolidation of Hinduism in Manipur. Then it was followed by the transformation of the whole social and political system of Manipur. He also established a theory of having a relationship between the members of the royal blood of Manipur and Babruvahan son of Arjun the hero of *Mahabharata.* It was also accept by the royal court. The name 'Ningthem' the traditional title given to the king was changed to 'Maharaja'.[63] The king was known as 'Manipureswar'.[64] In addition to this the king was given another name 'Gopal Das',[65] and Garibniwaz.[66] The name of the queen was also changed as Gomati Devi.[67]

To intensify the sanskritization process Santi Das introduced the Gotra for the seven salais or clans of the Meiteis.[68]

	Salai	*Gotra*
1.	Ningthouja (king's dynasty)	Shandilya
2.	Angom	Kaushika
3.	Chenglei (Sarang Leishangthem)	Bhardwaj
4.	Luwang	Kashyap
5.	Khuman	Madhugalya
6.	Moirang	Aitereya
7.	Khaba Nganba	Goutam

Then the king's dynasty which was founded by *Nongda Lairen Pakhangba* was declared equated with solar dynasty (Surya Bangsa) of Ramchandra of *Ramayana.* Perhaps this concept was formulated on the basis of a mythical tradition that Pakhangba was born of divine cloud egg from the sun which was presented to Leinung Yaibirok.

The identification of traditional festivals with Hindu festivals was also another important aspect in the sanskritization policy of Santi Das. He changed all the names of traditional festivals to Hindu name.[69]

Sl. No.	*Traditional Festival*	*Hindu Name*
1.	Heikru HidongbaAyang Yoiren Iruppa (Wakching) at Lilong	Jal Jatra Snan (Annual Bathing at Lilong Sahonpat
2.	Waira Tenkap Festival (Archery)	Kirtan of Lord Rama
3.	Poirei Apokma(In the month of Lamda)	Loipam Festival
4.	Kongba Leithong Phatpa (In the month of Sajibu)	Vishnu Sangkranti
5.	Ahong Khongching (In the month of Ingel)	Ratha Jatra
6.	Luklen Katpa (Offering to the ancestor in the month of Langban)	Tarpan (Offering to Petrilok)
7.	Wakamrog Chingnung Nongoubi (In the month of Mera)	Dussera Kwaktanba or Dussera
8.	Chanou Hui Chintu (New Harvest)	Goverdhan Puja

Introduction of social stratification among the people was also another developmental feature of the emergence of Hinduism among the Meiteis. In the very beginning the Meitei society was casteless society. But just after conversion to Hinduism, all the Meiteis are divided into several groups. The royal group was declared Kshetriyas. The Brahmins were formed as a separate group and non Hindus and other Shan or Buddhist group formed a separate social entity outside the Meitei society.[70] The introduction of the Hindu term'Rajkumar', which was addressed to all the members of royal blood was a distinctive evidence of the practice of social stratification and contribution of Santi Das for the division in the Meitei society. Introduction of the performing self-immolation at the death of their husband i.e. 'Sati' burning was also another feature of the introduction of the system of Hindu religious practices. Just after conversion many members of the royal family began to pilgrimage to several places of Hindu holy shrines under the guidance of Brahmin priest. This practice gave a very good room for having a regular cultural contact with the people of west. As a result of this of this new religious phenomenon a strong influence of Hindu way of life began to enter without any restriction into the Meitei society. Along with this under the influence of Santi Das the king of Manipur put so many instructions to the people. Under these new changes people were not allowed to eat meat. Eating meat was regarded as 'Mangba' i.e. unclean. Severe type of punishment was given to those persons who violated these new dietary rules.

Apart from this he also destroyed the abode of several traditional deities. The images were completely destroyed. These events are still popularly known as 'Kollu Yaikhaiba' (Destruction of the images of traditional deities). The conversion to Hinduism was also not voluntary. It was an act of forcible conversion. But nobody had the power to resist against it during his hey days. The anger of the people was clearly evidenced by the act of his own son Chit Sai. He had prosecuted the followers of Ramandi Cult. On the other hand if a close observation is to be made it can be suggested that the practice and concept of traditional religion was so strong that Vaishnavism made a compromise with it.[71] Therefore the system of Vaishnavism in Manipur may be treated as a kind of religious syncretism between Hinduism and traditional religion. This type new development in the religious practices was described as an outcome of the degree of religious fanaticism of the king.[72] Whatever the case may be Santi Das with the full support and cooperation of the iron hand policy of Garibniwaz had successfully planted and made grow the Hindu religious concept and practice on the soil of Manipur.

Emergence of Gouriya Vaishnavism

The emergence of Gouriya Vaishnavism or Bengal School of Vaishnavism was another important religious development in Manipur.

This religious concept and practice was initiated during the reign of Meidingoo Chingthangkhomba. Because of his deep religious devotion to Hinduism he was popularly known as Rajashri Bheigyachandra (Royal Saint).Bheigyachandra ruled Manipur twice. First from 1759 to 1762 and second from 1763 to 1798. During his period the concept of religious practices of Gouriya Vaishnavism was propagated by five religious monks. Their names were Ganganarayan Chakraverty, Krishnacharan Chakraverty, Krishnabihari, Nibiram Acharya and Ramgopal Beiragy.[73] One Ngangbam Selungba was the first person in the country who accepted the new religion. He was baptized by Ramgopal Beiragyi[74]. Other people who propagated the new religion were Ngangbam Krishnadas, Adhikari Kamdeva Brajabashi and Shri Rup Parmananda Thakur. King Bheigyachandra accepted the religious principles of Gouriya Vaishnavism from the hand of Shri Rup Parmananda Thakur.[75] Thus after accepting the *Gouriya Vaishnavism*, it became the state religion.

The influence of Gouriya Vaishnavism was further intensified by the installation of the image of Govindajee in the year 1776 and the subsequent religious and cultural programme, which was introduced by the king. The most noteworthy part in the whole process towards the installation of the image of Govinda was the event of taming of mad elephant in Assam by Bheigyachandra. Unfortunately in the chronicles of Assam, though the contribution of Kuranganayani, a Manipuri princess who married to the king of Assam was properly recorded, the event and action of the king of Manipur, which related with catching or taming of elephant was not reflected. But here in Manipur this particular event made a successful attempt to justify the action and policy of the installation of Govinda. This myth had greatly influenced the minds of the people and thus it gave a clear cut path for the establishment and consolidation Gouriya Vaishnavism. The installation of the wooden image of Govindajee was the most outstanding contribution of Bheigyachandra in the process of the consolidation of the Gouriya Vaishnavism. Another interesting part in the whole process was the establishment of relationship between the event of the taming of mad elephant in Assam and installation of the image. A story was constructed that king Bheigyachandra was able to capture the mad elephant with the help of Lord Krishna. Then after coming back from Assam king Bheigyachandra had forgotten the word of Lord Krishna. Then one day in his dream Lord Krishna asked him to make a statue in the exact form which was revealed to him in his dream. Lord Krishna further asked him to construct the image out of the jackfruit tree at the Kaina Hill. This powerful myth had turned the whole table of the mindset of the people in favour of the Gouriya Vaishnavism. And Lord Krishna was emerged in the minds of the people of Manipur as the only supreme deity of the creation of universe. This evidence clearly shows the wisdom and technique of the Hindu religion preacher in Manipur. Thus after having a brief discussion king Bheigyachandra went to Kaina Hill in search of jackfruit tree. After locating the jackfruit tree he gave reward to the members of Panganbam family for their help in the discovery of tree.[76] The wooden statue of Govinda, Gopinath, and Adietya was also installed. The four images of Krishna were worshipped at different places. Govinda was worshipped at Langthabal inside the palace compound. Bijoy Govinda under the care of Ananta Shai the uncle of the king at Sagolband. Adeitya was at Bishenpur and Gopinath by Shri Krittidhwaja of Ningthoukhong was given the title Kala Raja by the king. Thus the installation of Govindaji was a great significant development in the religious history of Manipur and it may be marked as a zenith in the process of the Hindu colonialism in the state.

The installation of the statue of Govindaji was followed by the establishment of wooden statue of 'Rasheswari'. The statue of Rasheswari was constructed by seven people. They were Kshetri Panem Nanda Singh, Konsaba Chakrapani, Konsaba Anindram, Konsaba Khelemba, Konsaba Haojou, Konsaba Samarok, Konsaba Yoiba.[77] For their successful effort to establish the statue the king gave them reward of three paris of agricultural land to each of them and one buffalo and one house worker.

The introduction of *Ras Leela*, a kind of religious dance, was another important feature of Gouriya Vaishnavism. Prof. Gangmumei said Manipuris worshipped God through dance and music.[78] These were the traditional practices right from the pre-historic period. But in this particular case a very interesting myth was created to justify the introduction of this dance form. It was mentioned that the composition of the Rass Leela was revealed through the dream of king Bheigyachandra. He introduced three types of Rass Leela *i.e.* Kunjarass, Maharass, and Basantarass. It is observed that the style of the composition of new form of dance is a combination of traditional Meitei dance form.[79] The degree of his devotion to Gouriya Vaishnavism was so great that he even dedicated the country to Lord Govinda and he ruled the state on his behalf. Because of his maximum degree of inclination to the new cult, the position of Brahmin was tremendously increased in the social strata of the country. It is also recorded that the king stepped down from the throne when one Brahmin was killed by a royal servant.

The emergence of Gouriya Vaishnavism of Bengal School of Vaishnavism was followed by the tremendous increase of the influence of Bengali culture in every aspects of the life of the people. Since most of the religious practices were from Bengal, their religious and cultural influence was reflected in every sphere of the life of the people. It brought a lot of changes in the dress, food habit and even in the practices of the religious rites. Such type of unprecedented development brought a complete domination of Bengali Brahmin on Manipuri society. Since Brahmins were regarded as a upper caste group they were exempted from the lallup duty and also exempted from cultivation. Apart from this under the patronage of the king they were allowed to do all types of religious activities in every villages. Temples were constructed with the support of the local people. These temples were used as the centre for religious propagation and feudal control agencies.[80] As a mark of honour and respect as upper caste group, people used to address them as 'Eigya'. Thus under the full protection of the king the Brahmins played as a dominant social group in every aspects of the life of the country.

Emergence of Brahma Sabha

The establishment of 'Brahma Sabha' as a highest apex body of the Brahmin group was a great noteworthy development in the history of the growth of Hindu religious authoritarianism in Manipur. The above mentioned facts have shown the importance of Hinduism in the state and role of the Hindu religious preachers. It is also a fact that during the period of king Bheigyachandra the process for the raise of Brahmin authoritarianism was completed with positive result and they dominated the whole social life of the state. The Brahmin group emerged as an important social group of the composite picture of the total population of Manipur. This new trend of development may be observed as the foundation for the establishment of 'Brahma Sabha'. It is said that before the installation of the image of Govinda in the year 1776 the religious institution was headed by a position called *'Hidang.*[81] But just after the installation of Govinda the whole administrative structure of the institution was changed and from the practice of individual headship the administration of Brahma Sabha was given to the responsibility of five positions. This was known as *'Pancha Ratan'*[82] (Five Ratan). Their names were (i) *Bidyalankar*, (ii) *Bidyanidhi*, (iii) *Bidyasunder*, (iv) *Bachaspati* and (v) *Bebyasthakari*. Along with the change of administrative structure this institution gradually began to involve, besides religion, to other social and cultural life of the people. Through their serious efforts the sanskritization process was effectively going on the social life of the state.

During the period of king Chourajeet (1803-1813) the number of position was again increased from five to nine. A new religious department was established as *'Naba Ratan'* (Nine Ratan).[83] The name of the position were (i) *Bebasthakari*, (ii) *Bachaspati*, (iii) *Bidyalangkar*, (iv) *Bidyanidhi*, (v) *Bidyasunder*, (vi) *Bidyabagesh*, (vii) *Tarkalangkar*, (viii) *Bamon Hanjaba* and (ix) *Bamon Hidang.*[84] Then during the period of Gambhir Singh (1825-1834) the nomenclature of this religion was widely known as 'Brahma Sabha'. The existence of the name 'Brahma Sabha' is mentioned in Cheitharol Kumbaba, the royal chronicle, in connection with a particular religious function.[85] But nothing is mentioned in any text about the change of the nomenclature of this religious institution to the present form. It is also said that the further consolidation of the religious principles and practices of Hinduism was made during the reign of king Chandrakirti Singh (1850-1886).[86] He further developed a religious book called 'Wayel Lairik' which was written during the period of Bheigyachandra mainly for the Meitei Hindu people. The name of the book was 'Byabasthanbarna'. The whole religious activities and any type of religious disputes were solved through this book.[87]

The most notable contribution of this religious organization to the society of Manipur was the introduction of the concept of ostracism. The local people called *'Mangba and Sengba'* (clean and unclean). The Brahma Sabha, with an objective to control the common people had framed some religious laws which were binding upon the people particularly Meitei Hindu. The religious rules of their organization declared that to meet mentally retarded persons or mad man, hill people, Muslims and Lois were the act of untouchable. Therefore Meitei Hindu people were forbidden to mix up with the hill people, Muslims and Lois.[88] Indeed, this particular provision of their religious laws may be observed as a deliberate attempt to create a dichotomy among different groups of people in the society of the country. This provision rendered on Himalayan contribution to create an undesirable effect in the equilibrium in the harmonious relationship among the different ethnic group. In addition to this there were a lot of contradiction and incoherentcy in other provisions also. It is mentioned that the common people were not allowed to marry girls from Brahmin community whereas the Brahmin boys can marry the girls from the common people after performing a particular religious rites. Such type of action of the organization has laid a basic foundation for the growth of unhappiness among the common people. In addition to this under their religious law the people coming from outside the state was declared untouchable. Therefore, the Meitei Hindu people were not allowed to mix up with them. If an individual violated this rule he was declared ostracized by the Brahma Sabha.

Such type of ostracism policy adopted by Brahma Sabha had created a serious social problem in the state. Fear psychosis was developed among the minds of the people. They were not able to work freely. Ultimately they became a prisoner under these draconian religious laws of the Brahma Sabha. Gradually the leaders of this organization became the most powerful person in the religious and social life of the state. They were able to do all these actions under the active patronage of the king. Even the king paid high respect to them. It is mentioned that even the king addressed to three leaders of the Brahma Sabha i.e. Bebhastakari, Acharya Guru and Rajpurohit with this word 'Nanai Ei' (I your servant).[89] Even the king perhaps thought that it was the duty of the king to accept their idea. At the same time there were a lot of contradictions in the implementation of their policy. It is also mentioned that if a person who was declared untouchable can be redeemed again after paying a fix amount of money. Such cases were happened in many instances. From these evidences it was observed that the real intention of the leaders of the Brahma Sabha was to establish a sanskritized society by adopting a various types of undesirable methods. And a large number of people became the victim of this law.

Thus, Hindu colonization process which was started from the period of king Kyamba (1467-1508) came to a complete form in the 18th century i.e. during the period of Bheigyachandra (1763-1798). During this long period the whole picture of the society of this state was completely transformed into the Hindu way of life. To see the active patronage of the king to the approach of the sanskritization process the people who were not in favour of this new religious changes, was not able to do any type of resistance action against the religious invasion forces. The people were forced to ignore the value of the traditional religious principles and practices. As a result of this the importance of the traditional religion which was associated with the growth of the society was completely sidelined and people began to give more emphasis to the practices of new religious cults. Accordingly a lot of new concepts and idea was developed in the minds of the people. From the strong influence of the Hindu preacher the people began to accept that they were the offshoots of the Aryan people. So, they began to give more importance to the religious sacred places of Hindu religion rather than the traditional religion. They began to claim that their genealogy starts from the time of Arjun, the hero of *Mahabharata* and it was also their belief that Manipur was associated with *Mahabharata*. As a mark of respect to the value of Hindu religion the people in their own initiative had constructed temples in every Meitei inhabited area and Brahmins were invited to make a permanent settlement and to manage the temple. The common people used to offer whatever the fruits and vegetables which were the first product of the season to the Hindu God. Then they also began to actively involve in every type of Hindu religious festivals. Gradually the Meitei people began to accept the concept of upper caste character of Brahmins and as a mark of respect the common people used to address them as 'Egya'.

Apart from this, as mentioned above, through religious practices the common people were greatly influenced by the customs of Hindu way of life. It gave influence particularly to the style of dress mainly to the Meitei man. The 'Dhoti' locally called 'Pheijom' and 'Kurta' locally called 'Pumyat' began to use extensively and to speak Bengali language was considered as a sign of educated people. They also accepted the idea of caste system, though it is not in the social system of the Meitei. Accordingly they began to respect the descendants of the king who is popularly known as 'Ningthemcha' (members of royal blood) and Brahmins as upper caste people. So, the common people began to address Ningthemcha as 'Sanakhya' like 'Eigya' to Brahmins. Thus the attempt of the Hindu religious preachers to make Manipur a completely sanskritised society was fulfilled very successfully in 18th century.

Then the introduction of the concept 'untouchable' by the Brahmin through a religious organization called 'Brahma Sabha' gave a new dimension to the outlook of the people. The introduction of so many conditions which were against the traditional social character of the state and imposition of these conditions to the people has created a breeding ground for the growth of unhappiness among the people.. Under this policy the common people began to get a lot of harassment and ultimately it became a social issue in the state. Therefore, the dominating character of the Brahmins in the social hierarchy of the state and their nature of relationship of high and low concept with common people had laid a basic foundation for the growth of the idea of religious revitalization movement in Manipur.

REFERENCES

1. Gangmumei Kamei, *History of Manipur*, vol. I, Pre-colonial period 1991. p.251.
2. R.C. Majumdar, *Hindu Colonialism,* 1973, p.8.
3. Dr. Hu Shih, *China and Western World*. p 16.
4. D.P. Singhal, *Buddhism in East Asia*. p.42.
5. *Ibid.,* p.52.
6. *Ibid.*
7. S. Sasanananda, *History of Buddhism in Assam* (300 B.C.-1200A), p.101.
8. Dhabala Singh, *An Outline History of Manipur*, p.25 Quoted in 'Meitrabak'. p.41.
9. D.P. Singhal, *op .cit.,* p.51.
10. R.C. Majumdar, *op. cit.*, p.8.
11. *Ibid.*.
12. H. Ibopishak Meitei, *Bamon Khunthoklon*, 1978, p.I.
13. R.K. Jhallajit, *A Short History of Manipur*, p.81.
14. H. Ibopishak Meitei, *op. cit.*, p.16.
15. N. Khelchandra & L. Ibungohal Singh, *Cheitharol Kumbaba*. p.19.
16. Gangmumei Kamei, *op. .cit.*, p.200.
17. Sarangthem Bormani, *Meitei Ningthourol,* 2000, p.46.
18. L. Ibungohal Singh, *Introduction to Manipur*, p.31.
19. H. Bijoy Singh, *Meitrabakki Wari*, p.74.
20. *Cheitharol Kumbaba*, p.102.
21. M. Kirti Singh, *Religious Development in Manipur in the 18th and 19th Century*, p.56.
22. H. Ibopishak Meitei, *op. cit.*, p.I.
23. *Ibid.*, pp.1-4.
24. *Ibid.*, pp.3-4.
25. R.K. Jhallajit Singh, *op. cit.*, p.62.

26. R.K. Sanahal, The Temple of Vishnu at Bishenpur (an article published in Manipuri Temple Architecture Bulletin No.3) August 1983 Mutua Museum, Imphal. pp.29-32.
27 Gangmumei Kamei, *op. cit.*, p.201.
28. *Ibid.*
29. *Ibid.*, p.201.
30. R.K. Jhallajit, *op. cit.*, p.84.
31. Gangmumei Kamei, *op. cit.*, pp.238-239.
32. T.C. Hodson, The Meitheis. p.95.
33. H. Ibopishak Meitei, *op. cit.*, p.12.
34. *Ibid.*
35. *Ibid.*, pp.10-12.
36. *Cheitharol Kumbaba*, p.68.
37. R.K. Jhallajit, *op. cit.*, p.115.
38. H. Ibopishak, *op. cit.*, p.12.
39. *Cheitharol Kumbaba*, p.70.
40. T.C. Hodson, *The Meitheis*. p.95.
41. *Cheitharol Kumbaba*, p.73.
42. H. Ibopishak, *op. cit.*, pp.14-15.
43. *Cheitharol Kumbaba*. p.76.
44. *Ibid.*, p.76.
45. R.K. Jhallajit, p.134.
46. *Ibid.*
47. At that time Manipur was known by different name.
48. O. Bhogeshwar Singh, *Sanamahi Laikan*. 2nd Ed., 1995. p.48.
49. *Ibid* ., p.50.
50. *Cheitharol Kumbaba*, p.83.
51. Sylvian gods presiding over villages and lineages.
52. *Cheitharol Kumbaba*, p.84.
53. *Ibid.*, p.85.
54. P. Sunder, *Sakok Lamlen*. p.9 Moirangamba and K. Kumar.
55. *Cheitharol Kumbaba*, p.93.
56. Kh. Kaomacha Singh, *Manipuri Ittibritti*, 1934, p.68.
57. Atombapu Sharma, *Pakhangba*, 1952 , pp.4-5.
58. Gangmumei Kamei, *op. cit.*, p.255.

59. *Ibid.*
60. *Cheitharol Kumbaba,* p.89.
61. *Ibid.,* p.90.
62. *Ibid.*
63. *Ibid,* p.85.
64. Sanamahi Laikan, p.50.
65. *Ibid.,* p.61.
66. *Ibid.,* p.50.
67. *Ibid.*
68. *Ibid.,* p.59-60.
69. *Ibid.,* pp.63-64.
70. Gangmumei Kamei, p.258.
71. *Ibid,* p.259.
72. *Ibid.*
73. R.K. Sanahal, Manipurda Vaishnav Dharmagi Ehou (An article) Manipur Rajya Hindu Sanmelon-1981.
74. *Ibid.*
75. *Ibid.*
76. *Cheitharol Kumbaba,* p.129.
77. R.K. Sanahal, *op. cit.,* pp.
78. Gangmumei Kamei, *op. cit.,* p.276.
79. *Ibid.,* p.
80. *Ibid.,* p.279.
81. N. Ibochouba Singh, A. Chitreshwar Singh, B. Kullachandra Singh, *Meitei Bamon Hourakpham* (*Beginning of Meitei Bamon*), 1995, p.6.
82. *Ibid.,* p.7.
83. *Ibid.*
84. *Ibid.*
85. *Cheitharol Kumbaba,* p.238.
86. Sairem Nilbir, *Laiyingthou Sanamahi Amasung Sanamahi Laining Hingat Ihou.,* 2002. p.160.
87. Dr. M. Kirti Singh, Meitei Bamon Amasung Brahmasabhagi Houraklon (A Manipur article published in *'Khongthang'* 35 No. April/May, 1981.
88. *Ibid.*
89. Sairem Nilbir, *op. cit.,* p.162.

4

Apokpa Marup

The emergence of *Apokpa Marup* in the year 1930 as a socio-religious organisation with a great radical objective to bring a complete transformation in the life of the people was a great landmark in the process of the historical development of Manipur. On the other hand the establishment of this organisation was a big significant step towards the growth of the idea of religious revitalization movement in the state and in other neighbouring areas. The birth of this organisation was directly related with the existing religious practices of Hinduism and chauvinistic attitude of the Brahmins towards the common people. Such type of attitude was treated by some people as a religious colonization policy of the Brahmins. From this aspect the emergence of '*Apokpa Marup*' was a great watershed in the ongoing process of the entire religious, social, cultural and even the political life of the people of Manipur. Through the platform of this organisation, the people were able to get the opportunity to understand many inside aspects of the existing religious practices which was not in the minds of the people for quite long time and its impact in the social and economic life of the country as a whole. From this platform the people began to know both the positive and negative sides of the religious practices of the Hindu way of life in the society. Indeed, the establishment of this organisation was a great breakthrough to the ongoing historical development particularly in the religious and cultural life of the people because it promoted an idea for the growth of the concept of self-identity among the people particularly the younger generation of the society. Ultimately it rendered a good help in the process of recalling the glory and pride which was enjoyed by the people before the coming of Hinduism.

One great personality called Naoria Phullo was the heart and soul for the establishment of this organisation. At his initiative and leadership this organization was able to occupy a unique position in the religious history of this place. Due to his sacrificial attitude and noble character he was lovingly addressed by his disciples and admirers as 'Lainghal' (Head of religious organization). With the help of his analytical observations the people particularly of younger generation was able to launch a successful religious movement in Manipur and other adjoining areas. Naoria Phullo was born on 28th August 1887[1] at Jaribon in Cachar District Assam. He was the grandson of Naorem Herando who was the founder of Naorem family at Laishram Khul in Cachar. His father's name was Chaoba and mother's name was Thambou. He started his early educational career from a lower primary school at Rajespur. He was a boy of charming personality and having an attractive smiling face. To see his innocent and smiling facial nature his teachers lovingly called him 'Phool' means flower. From this word later on he was popularly known as 'Phullo'[2]. Just after the completion of lower and middle primary schooling he continued his study at Heilakandi High School. His father died when he was only in class eighth standard. In the year 1914 he passed Entrance Examination and became a teacher at Heilakandi High School. From here he went to Lata M.E. School and became the Assistant Head Master. In the 1916 he joined the state service of the Government of Assam and posted at the office of the Deputy Commissioner, Silchar. Then in the year 1917 he again joined the state police service as Sub Inspector and his first posting was at Dibrugarh. Thus, for a considerable period of time he was in the Government's service and during this period he was able to earn a lot of wonderful experience and knowledge which rendered a great help in his future course of action. It is said that he had a habit of strong tendency to understand the minds of the people of different communities. Accordingly he always tried to mix up with the people of various groups of people. From this experience he was able to understand the minds and attitude of other people towards the people of Manipur. The negative attitude and ideas of superiority complex of other group of people towards Manipuris might have been a great influential factor for him to the growth of a new idea for the establishment and promotion of a distinctive identity of the Manipuri people. It is also mentioned that his idea to foster the historical identity of Manipuri people was strongly motivated by two important incidents. The first incident was occurred in the month of March of the year 1927. On a particular day of this month Naoria Phullo had come across a Manipuri old man on the road of a hill area at Rangia.[3] He was absolutely overwhelmed by the fantastic analytical observation of the old man on the religious and social position of the people of Manipur. Ultimately it gave a new idea for the promotion of the traditional cultural and religious life of the people of Manipur. The nature of the second incident was not clearly spelled out but it is said that this incident encouraged him to do something concrete for the preservation of distinctive national identity of Manipuri people.

Naoria Phullo was of the view that the undesirable negative attitude of other groups of people towards Manipuris was mainly due to her existing religious practices of Hinduism which was introduced by the Brahmins. Since it was brought from outside some people made an attempt to put in the category of cargo cult. After examining the whole picture of the social life of the people under the principles of new religion he strongly asserted that the distinctive identity of Manipuris could be well protected only when the traditional religious principles and practices were fostered very effectively. Thus after getting a ray of convincing idea he started to campaign with a forceful argument for the promotion of the historical identity of the people. Indeed, it was a very significant step in the developmental process for the preservation of the national identity of the Manipuris. Another important contribution of this new developmental idea was that it gave a direct challenge to the practices of Hindu religion and also to the hegemonistic and authoritative nature of Brahma Sabha, the highest apex body of Hindu religion in Manipur. For this noble cause he received a lot of sufferings even from his own society. People started to treat him as an atheist and many people began to criticise his radical concept as an action of utopianism. However, Naoria Phullo did not pay much heed to the negative criticism of the people because he was fully aware that he could bring a complete transformation through his positive thinking. Indeed, to give an open confrontation to the religious authoritative power of Brahma Sabha in such a peculiar situation was a great challenging task of Naoria Phullo. At that particular period of time nobody had the power to speak anything against the chauvinistic attitude of this religious organization as they were strongly supported by the king of Manipur. Therefore to see this entire possible dangerous outcome from the ruling elite, even the nearest relatives of Naoria Phullo did not appreciate his action. However in the midst of these hurdles Naoria Phullo continued the activities of his mission with full enthusiasm. Thus with tireless efforts he was able to lay a big foundation to foster the national identity of the people of this state.

It is very interesting to note that Naoria Phullo, though he had strongly advocated for the promotion of traditional religious concept and practices, never made any type of frontal attack to the basic philosophy of Hindu religion. The whole thesis of his arguments was based not on the basic principles and concept of Hindu religion but on the economic life of the people which was emerged just after the emergence of Hinduism. He was of the view that the suffering of the people particularly in the financial life was mainly due to the outcome of the practices of Hindu religion. From the nature and religious policy of Brahmins he was of the opinion that their only objective was nothing but to squeeze the economic life of the people through religious practices. So he strongly deplored the continuous efforts of the Brahmins to destroy the distinctive identity of the Manipuri people. He was of the view that the Brahmins exploited the economic life of the people by using religious tools. Besides, he also strongly criticized the social discrimination policy of Brahmins.

He said that their new social policy led to the growth of any type of disturbances in the social equilibrium of the country. From all these angles Naoria Phullo was of the view that the ignorance for the cause of the indigenous people and idea of social ostracism policy was a deliberate attempt of the Brahmins to subdue the raising intellectual power of the people of Manipur.[5] To see all these undesirable developments in the social and religious life of the people, Phullo thought that to bring a mutual awareness among the common people was the only remedy to this unhealthy environment. With this sole objective and in order to give a new idea to the people he wrote a number of books in which he pointed out the negative impact of the religious policy of the Brahmins. He always asserted that the religious policy of the Brahmins was the most important reason for growth of the confusing situation in the national identity of the people of Manipur. So to give a new outlook to the people he gave an account of the historical process of the establishment of the religious colonization policy of the Brahmins in Manipur. In his celebrated work '*Eigi Wareng*' (My Prose) he gave a convincing observation about the nature of the religious colonisation policy of the Brahmins. Apart from this he also made a successful attempt to give the real identity of the Brahmins who entered in Manipur. At the same time he was also able to give a vivid picture of the real intention of the Brahmins in the cultural and economic life of the people. In his thesis he tried to establish an argument that the only intention of the Brahmins was to destroy the economic life and foundation of the people of Manipur through religious means. From this aspect many people regarded his work as the 'Magna Carta' in the process for the promotion of the traditional religious practices and principles. To make it more precise in his attempt to justify the reason for the establishment of 'Apokpa Marup' as a platform for giving awareness among the common people Phullo also made a critical observation of the nature of the Brahmins and their religious practices introduced in the several social occasions.

The nature and existing conditions for the growth of large scale influx of Brahmins in Manipur has already been mentioned in the previous chapter. Naoria Phullo observed that Brahmins entered Manipur due to the continuous harassment from the Muslim rulers in other parts of India. It was mainly because of their religious contradiction. Under this policy the Hindu people got a lot of trauma. So in order to get themselves free from any type of possible danger they fled to the different directions particularly in the eastern side. Ultimately they also reached Manipur. At their request the king of Manipur permitted them to make their settlement here and he even allowed them to marry the local girls as their wife. Apart from this the king also gave them a separate family name. Thus they were absorbed into the social fabric of the life of Meitei people. Taking the advantage of the liberal and sympathetic nature of the king and also after getting strong patronage from the king, the Brahmin people began to develop certain degree of superiority complex in their mind. Accordingly they began to take the indigenous people as a lower category people. Naoria Phullo said the emergence of this superiority complex among the Brahmins was the ultimate factor for the creation of problem in the equilibrium of the society. Because of this idea of superiority concept they tried to distance themselves from the people of this place. They refused to eat anything prepared by the non-Brahmins. This new phenomenon was not a happy development among the people. By recalling the history of the nature of treatment meted out to them by the Muslims, Naoria Phullo said that there was a lot of inconsistency in the character of the Brahmin group. He further observed that in some particular period of time they even compromised their conservative religious principles in order to make adjustment with the nature of cultural and social life of the Muslim community[6] and so some of the Brahmins might have been the offshoots of the Muslims[7]. From the platform of this observation Phullo raised a question on how the Brahmins, who had already compromised their religious principles and practices with another community whom they always regarded as an untouchable section, could claimed themselves as a higher group of people in Manipur. They were the offshoots of Manipuri women and at the same time they were also the son-in-laws of the Meities. He even extended his observation in such a way that as they were the sons of the Manipuri women they should not be treated as pure Brahmins. This new concept of superiority in the man to man relationship had produced another interesting phenomena *i,e*, the son-in-laws became the Gurus of father-in-laws[9] and pure became impure and impure became pure.[10]

Naoria Phullo strongly asserted that the basic motive of the Brahmins was to reduce the growing strength of the Meitei people. Therefore in order to materialize their objective into reality they had adopted various types of religious practices which give serious psychological effects to the people. The introduction of *Nongkhrang Iruppa* (Diving into the water with Nongkhrang- a kind of tree) system was a wonderful device of the preachers of new religion through which the common people were forced to accept the Hindu religion and its way of life. Under this system the people, as a mark of acceptance to embrace the new religion had immersed into the water with a branch of Nongkhrang tree in their hand. It was also believed that once a person had performed this ritual it indicates that he or she accepted to keep their allegiance to the new religion. It is said that people were not willing to embrace the new religion. But they were forced by the king to perform this ritual as a mark of acceptance of the new religion. This particular system and event was always regarded by the radicalist people as the beginning of the growth of laziness in the character and nature of the people of this state in general. This tendency of laziness is locally known as *Anam Aha Chuba*. Naoria Phullo said that the degree of laziness which was developed just after the acceptance of Hinduism was so severe that it rendered a great contribution in the process of the growth of deteriorating economic condition of the people. He further said that the declining conditions in the economic life of the country was created by three important reasons *i.e.* (a) decline of the degree and power of intellect of the people (b) lack of sincere efforts to improve the knowledge and (c) decline of the economic capabilities of the people. Therefore he was of the view that such type of unhealthy environment in the developmental process of the country was due to the new religious system.

The introduction of caste system in the social life of the people of Manipur was also another contribution of the introduction of new religion. This type of new phenomenon was an unprecedented experience in the life of the state. The creation of the upper and lower categories of social group had created serious effects in the equilibrium of the society which was enjoyed by the people from time immemorial. On the other hand it is also observed that this new concept rendered a great help to the Brahmins in their deliberate attempt to exploit the indigenous people of this place. Under this system the indigenous people were forced to accept their social status as a second grade in their own motherland. Actually the introduction of the concept of caste system had seriously affected the moral of the indigenous people of Manipur. The treatment meted out by the Brahmins to the people as an untouchable section had produced a negative effect in the man to man relationship in the society which was never experienced by the people. On the other hand it is also observed that this new concept rendered a great help to the Brahmins in their consistent attempt to exploit the indigenous people. But they were able to do it very successfully simply because they were supported by the ruler.

Phullo also deplored the practice of social discrimination introduced by the religious preachers between the indigenous people and Brahmins. In this respect he pointed out the nature of idol worshipping which was introduced by them. According to this existing system the Hinduised local people were not allowed to worship the idol by touching its body. Whereas the Brahmins made no restriction. Indeed such type of opportunity was reserved only for the Brahmins. Such type of policy of the Brahmins was regarded by Phullo as an act of irony and contradictory on their part. He said with the help of the ruler they forced the local people to embrace Hinduism and on the other hand the same group of people did not permit the local people to worship the idol by touching its body. To worship of Hindu god by touching the body of the statue was reserved only for the Brahmins who considered themselves as the upper caste people. This is a good evidence of social discrimination policy introduced by

Brahmins. Apart from this they also introduced a kind of salutation which was claimed as the highest form of the degree of modesty or humbleness. According to this system the common people have to prostrate at the feet of the Brahmins as a mark of respect to their social status. The introduction of such type of system was observed by Naoria Phullo as a part of systematic exploitation of the local people and it seriously effected to the moral courage of the Manipuri people. Thus gradually the Brahmin began to introduce Hindu way of life in the food habit, dress etc.etc Thus with the introduction of various types of religious practices in the social and cultural life of the people the Brahmin superiority over the indigenous people had increased tremendously and in every inch of their religious and social life the Brahmin became an indispensable social element. Due to this growing situation the superiority of Brahmin had developed in the social hierarchy of the country. Thus the superiority concept of the Brahmins and their attitude to the indigenous people is one of the most important factors for the growth of unhappiness among the people and it made a room for the growth of undesirable situation in the religious life in the state in near future.

As already mentioned above about the strong assertion of Naoria Phullo in regard to the systematic economic exploitation carried out by the Brahmins through the religious tools. This was clearly evidenced by the religious practices introduced by the Brahmins and nature and degree of the involvement of money to be incurred by the common people. But the common people were not able to understand all these growing situation because they were all hypnotized by the Brahmins. From this point of view he strongly asserted that the real motive of the introduction of such type of undisguised form of economic exploitation was nothing but to put a checkmate to the rising level of economic and intellectual power of the indigenous people of Manipur. So the application of Hindu religious practices in the social and cultural life of the people also one of the contributing factor for the growth of the idea of self identity.

Phullo also pointed out that the Brahmins of other areas did not pay much respect to the Brahmins of Manipur. He was of the view that the adoption of Hindu religious principles and practices by the Meiteis and adoption of Manipuri language by the Brahmins as their mother tongue perhaps might be the reason for the development of this idea. But he strongly expressed his unhappiness to the submissive attitude of Meitei people towards the Brahmins. By recalling the heroic deeds of the Meitei people in the past Naoria Phullo lamented that all the energies and capabilities were completely liquidated just after the embracement of Hindu religion. The moment they bowed down at the feet of Brahmins all their strength and courage was vanished once for all. Such type of development in the nature of social and religious behavior of Meitei people was regarded by Phullo in the following words, i.e. "Born with full growth stage, to get mangy at the stage of teen age, to become insane at the stage of youth and finished their old age with folk stories".[11]

Cyclical Rituals

Cyclical ritual means the religious rites which were performed by every society under certain beliefs during the life time of an individual. Birth, marriage, death etc. are the main religious ceremonies performed by every society in a cyclist way. Manipur also had enjoyed the cyclical rituals in a very systematic way according to their belief under the concept and practices of their indigenous religion. The observation of Naoria Phullo was that under the religious practices of Hinduism all the beauties of their religion and distinctive rites and rituals of the society were completely destroyed. Rather under the new religious practices the Brahmins exploited the economic life of the indigenous people.

Birth Ceremony

To give birth of a new child is an important positive aspect not only to the members of the family but also to the whole society because they would constitute the members of the new generation and ultimately they were the future pillars of the society. Therefore every members of the family always took proper utmost care and attention to the newly born children. So apart from their physical care the members of the family also took help from the God by performing the religious rites and rituals right from the moment of the birth of the children. Like other social groups the indigenous people of Manipur also had enjoyed certain rites and rituals in connection with birth ceremonies under their traditional religion. Along with this so many taboos were also practiced with an objective to keep proper care both mother and newly born baby. Under this practice both mother and newly born baby were not allowed to go outside the room for six days. On this very day a religious ceremony is performed which is locally known as 'Tarukni Ipan Thaba'. This ritual is performed with the help of 'Maibi' (midwife). It is a long process which started from the morning with the birth of mother and newly born baby. Then it is followed by certain rituals and rites like to give religious hymns to the newly born baby by their father and thus these rituals continued till evening. In this long process there is no room for heavy financial expenditure.

But just after the introduction of Hindu religious way of life and rituals the traditional name of *'Tarukni Ipan Thaba'* was replaced by the Sanskrit word *'Swasthi Puja'.* The ritual was performed with the help of Brahmins. Along with this change a myth was also created by the preachers of new religion that on this particular day a god called *Vidhi* would come to write the fortune of the newly born baby. It is not very clear whether there is a god called *Vidhi* among the list of gods under the Hindu mythology. But under the influence of the Brahmins the local people called this unknown feature as *Vidhi* or *Vidhata.* Accordingly a big religious practices was arranged to perform this puja. The only concern of Naoria Phullo was the involvement of heavy expenditure in the name of religion. The ceremony started with an item called *Potyengba.* Under this system the family of mother's side has to bring a number of items. To purchase these items the family of mother's side spend a large amount of money. There was no limit in the degree of the quantity of items. It depends on the number of invitation. Some of the important items which is meant only for newly born children are mattress (*Mompak*), pillow (*Mon*) and other related clothes with these items. These articles would be carried by the parents of mother's side to the house where the birth ceremony is performed. This system is called *Potyengba*. Then in the late evening the Brahmin performed *Swasthi Puja* and as a part of this religious ritual the family arranged refreshment for all the people who gathered there at their invitation. It was also made compulsory for all the invitees to pay certain amount of money to the newly born baby. This system is known as *Dan thadaba i.e.*, to offer charity. This system was not enjoyed by the people under the traditional religious practices. Thus under these new religious rituals the whole attention and importance is placed in the evening functions where heavy financial expenditure is involved. Naoria Phullo said that this new transformation was nothing but to introduce a new policy with an objective to exploit the financial condition of the indigenous people and to make a way for the improvement of the economic condition of Brahmins.[11]

Death Ceremony

Every ethnic group has their own distinctive characteristic features of death ceremony. Before the introduction of the present system the people of Manipur had practiced a distinctive feature according to their traditional system. It is recorded that in a particular stage of time the people of this place had practiced four types of disposal of death body. They were (1) Air cremation, (2) Water cremation, (3) Buried system of cremation, and (4) Fire cremation.[12] However, in course of time the disposal of death bodies in the air, water and buried system was discontinued. However, the system of water cremation and disposal of death bodies in the air was continued in a different form. The water cremation system was practiced as a severe type of punishment to those persons who committed crimes or acted against desire of the king and disposal of death body in the air was practiced to those persons who died in an unnatural death like hanging by themselves (Thouri Yanba).The evidences of buried system are clearly shown by the archaeological findings. It is mentioned that the fire cremation system was introduced in the year 1724 A. D.[13] *i.e.* during the reign of King Garibniwaz. Under the Hindu religious practices the rituals of death ceremony is continued for the whole year. First fifteen or sixteen days from the death of a person the bereaved family has performed a hectic religious programme. Then it was followed by the observation of monthly religious rites along with feast and it was continued till the annual death ceremony (*Phiroy*) is performed. The performance of rituals was started immediately just from the day of the cremation of the death body. It was followed by *Asthi Sanchay* or *Asthi Loukhatpa*, which is performed five or six days after the death of person according to the difference in the status of sex. Under this ritualistic principle apiece of bone of the death body which was removed from the forehead at the time of cremation was cleaned by the nearest relative of the deceased person. Then it was taken either to the bank of a nearby river or pool. It was followed by some rituals and from there the bone was carried by the nearest relative with a religious procession to the house. Then it was followed another big ritual called *Sorat Sonba*. It is mentioned that this word 'Sorat' may be a corrupted form of the word 'Shradha'. It is perhaps either a Sanskrit or Bengali word. Indeed, the *Shradha* Ceremony is a very important part in the whole religious process of the death ceremony. Naoria Phullo said such type of ritual is quite similar with the traditional practice called *Chuk Saba*.[15] It is also a traditional religious practice. But now this practice is confined only to those who died in an unnatural way.

By pointing out the real system of the Shrradha ceremony under the Hindu religious practices Naoria Phullo said this ritual is performed according to the guide line of a religious book named *Prayog Chintamani*.[16] According to his observation there were a sharp contradiction between the nature of the religious practices mentioned in the book and the system introduced by the Brahmins. One of his critical observations was the financial part involved in this ritual. He said the guide line did not mention anything extravagant which might cause a great financial problem to the bereave members of the family. The book mentioned only sixteen items which were the basic requirements in the process of the performance of the death ceremony. The items were: 1.Earth (*Bhumi*) 2. Seat (*Ashan*) 3. Water (*Jal*) 4. Perfume (*Gandha*) 5. Lamp (*Dip*) 6.Rice (*Anna*) 7. Cloth (*Bastra*) 8. Vegetable (*Tambul*) 9. Fruit (*Fal*) 10. Flower (*Pushpa*) 11. Gold

(*Kanchan*) 12. Umbrella (*Satra*) 13.Silver (*Rajat*) 14. Cot (*Sheija*) 15. Cow (*Go*) and 16. Chapple (*Peduka*).[17] It is also mentioned that these items would be presented to the Brahmin who were treated under the religious belief as the representative of the ancestors of the deceased person. And in a symbolic way a leaf of *Kusha* plant represents the Brahmin. It is also mentioned that if the members of the bereaved family were not able to get the articles mentioned above it can be replaced by the price value. From these facts Naoria Phullo said that the real nature of *Shradha Ceremony* and its nature of practices did not make any additional room for a heavy financial burden to the members of the bereave family. But the problem was, according to Phullo that the Brahmins did not follow the exact guideline and religious practices mentioned in the book. There were a lot of serious contradiction between the guideline and practices introduced by the Brahmins in the state of Manipur. He further said that this new trend of religious practices which was observed outside the framework of the religious book was nothing but to introduce a system for the exploitation of economic life of the state. Such type of nature of exploitation, according to Phullo, was started right from the day of the death of the person. Just after the process of cremation was completed the family members of the deceased person invited a Brahmin to perform certain ritual connected with the death of person which the local people used to call it *Lairik Taba* (to hear the verse of religious book). This system is continued till the previous day of the *Shradha Ceremony*. As a part of the religious norms the members of the family have to provide certain items for those people who have come to attend the function. Naoria Phullao was of the view that whatever it may be but this system which was introduced by the Brahmins have created a room for an additional expenditure of the deceased family. He said that this practice was not mentioned in any Hindu religious book which is connected with death ceremony. On the basis of this observation Phullo said that the introduction of this system is a serious contradiction to what was mentioned in their religious book.

In regard to the nature of the observation of the *Shradha Ceremony* Naoria Phullo was of the view that the new trend of religious rituals which was introduced by the Brahmins was a serious contradiction to the real guideline. He said that under this new system the members of the bereaved family got little time to mourn the death of the person. Their mind and energy was confined mainly to the issue of how to meet the process of preparation of the various programmes and items of articles to be purchased. He said these processes were made compulsory deliberately by the Brahmins for their own benefit. For the rich and well to do families the degree of the amount of expenditure incurred by them might not be a problem but for the members of the poor families it was a great problem. On the other side an impression was forced to develop in the minds of the people that if the death ceremony was performed in a symbolic way they would get a very bad impression from the public. So out of the fear from the possible negative impression of the public even the members of the poor families also tried to arrange in a large scale way by utilizing any type of means. Sometimes they were forced by the circumstances to sale even their immovable property. On the other hand an impression was also made among the people that if the death ceremony was performed to the best satisfaction of the general people the spirit of the departed soul would get peace in the heavenly abode.

Another interesting aspect was that out of these sixteen items which are required for the performance of death ceremony as mentioned in the *Prayog Chintamani* the members of the bereaved family always kept attention to five specific items. They are 1. *Ashan Dan* (Charity of Seat), 2. *Jal Dan* (Charity of Water) 3.*Anna Dan* (Charity of rice), 4. *Basta Dan* (Charity of cloth) and 5. *Sheija Dan* (Charity of cot). Naoria Phullo said these five items have created a serious financial burden to the members of the bereaved family. And it became a general problem to every Manipuri people.[18] Actual problem faced by the people was that when they arranged these items they have added so many additional articles. For example in the case of the preparation of *Ashan* Dan(Seat charity) the people added some additional items like *Hidakphu Makhong* (stand of smoking organ), *Nganthak* (The bowl of hookah), *Cheisu* (staff or walking stick) etc. Naoria Phullo said the inclusion of these additional items was not mentioned in any of the Hindu religious books. The idea to include these articles was nothing but to create an environment deliberately by the Brahmins to face a financial burden to the members of the bereaved family[19] and ultimately it has become a general concern of all the people of this state. In the case of *Jal Dan* (water charity) also some kind of extravagant arrangement was made by the common people. Here the members of the bereaved family used a big jar for water. Usually people for religious purposes used jar made of brass metal. It was very costly and it was not easily available in the market. Since the use of big jar in the religious function was made compulsory the people always took it as an obligatory on their part. Therefore people were trying to get it at any cost. The same pattern was also practiced in the system of *Gandha Dan* (perfume charity). As mentioned in the religious book *Gandha Dan* could be done in a symbolic way by using flower. But in the case of the present practice the people have to purchase the best quality of perfume oil. In the same way in the system of *Anna Dan* (Rice Charity) also the people put a large quantity of rice along with various items of vegetables. Apart from this the people also added all the requisite cooking materials. Thus every members of the bereaved family have spent a huge amount of money. In fact such type of practice was a serious contradiction to the beautiful idea of symbolic representation mentioned in the religious books. The same system was also continued in the preparation of *Basta Dan* (charity of cloth) item. It is mentioned that in order to give charity the members of the bereaved family always tried to get the same quality of cloth which was used by the deceased person when he was alive. In this respect an impression was developed in the minds of the people that all these clothes which was used in the death ceremony would be used by the deceased person in the heavenly abode. This idea, according to Phullo, was injected in the minds of the common people by the Brahmins with an objective to give additional financial burden in the name of the religion.

The most expensive area in the preparation of the items of death ceremony was the arrangement of *Sheija Dan* (Cot charity). Under a certain belief the members of every bereaved family prepared this item with utmost care. In the process of the preparation of this item people added so many additional items which they considered as a part of the *Sheija Dan.* The items are:- (a) mattress, (b) pillow, (c) mosquito net, (d) purdah, (e) wearing cloths,(f) cloths, (g) cooking utensils and (h) money for every items. Naoria Phullo said that the above mentioned additional articles are not mentioned in that religious book. The people simply arranged it at the directive of the Brahmins. But on the other side the value of the expenditure was so heavy that sometimes even the people of rich family faced the financial problem. However the people continued this practice as they believed that if they performed the death ritual ceremony to best satisfaction of the people and Brahmins the soul of the departed body would be able to live peacefully in the heaven.

Another aspect of the *Shradha Ceremony* is the performance of *Sankirtan* by group singers. The religious ceremony starts with the chanting of hymns by the Brahmins in the place of *Puja* and then it was followed by *Sankirtran.* It is also made compulsory of the members of the deceased family to prepare different type of long cloth for all the persons who were in the singing party. This system provides another room to the family to meet extra expenditure. Then it was followed by refreshment for all the people who come to attend the death ceremony. Therefore to meet all these requisite expenditure the members of the deceased family have to arrange a sizeable amount of money. Phullo said this type of development was indeed a big problem for all the people. But mainly due to the existing environment the people were not able to speak out openly. And the circumstances compelled them to follow the directive of the religious authority.

Based on the ground reality Naoria Phullo also pointed out another interesting aspect of the *Shradha Ceremony.* It has already stated above about the inner religious idea of the articles or items prepared by bereaved family. The members of the deceased person arranged all these with the idea that with the help of these requisite items the departed soul would be able to live peacefully in the heavenly abode.

On the other hand the religious book did not mention anything on the question of whom would receive all the charity items of the ceremony. But as a practice all the charity items were received by the Brahmin who performed the religious rites and rituals of the ceremony. No direct members or even the relatives of the members of the bereave family were not entitled to receive any article of the ceremony. According to this convention just after the rituals was completed all the charity items were sent to the residence of the said Brahmin. Whereas in the case of the *Shradha Ceremony* of the Brahmin families all the charity items were received only by the nearest relatives of the bereave family. This is also one of the areas where Naoria Phullo severely criticized and he regarded it as a discriminative policy of the Brahmins. The introduction of two types of contradictory religious practices, according to him, was nothing but to lay a foundation stone to exploit the financial life of the common people and on the other hand this arrangement makes a room for the improvement of the financial condition of the Brahmin family. He further said that it clearly indicates the highest degree of the undesirable characters of the Brahmins in their approach. He also strongly asserted the injustices committed by the Brahmins to people in the state of Manipur. He was of the view that such type of policy adopted deliberately in the name of the religion had rendered a great contribution in the process of the strengthening of their social and economic condition in this state. They were able to make a successful attempt at the cost of the life of the indigenous people. Thus Naoria Phullo, based on the basis of ground reality, was able to portrait the policy and characters of Brahmins in a more effective way.

This is not the end of the process of death ceremony. The *Shradha Ceremony* was followed by the memorial feast which was organized every month by the family of the deceased person. The basic objective of this feast was to remember the deceased person. This system was continued for eleven months. Just after the end of these months the family again organized an annual feast which is known as *Phiroi.* This ritual is also performed in a large scale way along with *Sankirtan* and some charity items. The items were cloths, utensils, mattresses and vegetables etc. Like *Shradha ceremony* all the charitable items have taken to the residence of the Brahmin who performed the rituals.

Another interesting aspect is the concept of the program of pilgrimage by the members of the deceased person. Actually it is not a compulsory on the part of the death ceremony. But it is the common impression of all the people that the death ritual is not completed until and unless the piece of the bone of the forehead of the died person immersed into the water body of the river Ganga which is considered by every Hindu people as a sacred religious place. This impression and concept was created by the Brahmins in Manipur. Therefore under this belief the people of this area always make an attempt to go on pilgrimage just after the end of annual feast *Phiroy*. Thus in order to go pilgrimage people has arranged a large amount of money. Their belief was so strong that even if they were not able to get the requisite amount of money without having any hesitation they borrowed money from the other people with interest. The ultimate outcome was that if they were not able to clear within that stipulated time they were forced by the situation to sell their immovable property. Thus in the name of the religion most of the people got severe type of financial harassment.

After analyzing the nature of the religious practices of the death ceremony Naoria Phullo gave a critical observation by saying that the hidden agenda of the Brahmins might be to squeeze the financial position of the indigenous people of this state. Under this system people found no room where they did not spend money. On the other hand, perhaps under some certain impression, people sometimes made a huge amount of expenditure in the performance of death ceremony. In such cases the Brahmins did not make any attempt to stop the possibilities of over expenditure. Rather very silently they encouraged such type of phenomenon. From this angle Naoria Phullo said that such type of the observance of death ceremony under the Hindu religious way, as introduced by Brahmins, is highly coloured by the character and nature of 'festive mood' rather than the manner of the mourn of died person.

Introduction of Religious Festivals

The introduction of religious festivals with the strong patronage of the king was also regarded by the people of radicalist section of the society as an important factor for the growth of the deteriorating condition in the economic life of the people of Manipur. It is a historical fact that right from the primitive period the people of this place worshipped god through dance and various type of music. Therefore dance is a part not only in the cultural life of the people but it also played a predominant role in the religious functions of the state. But just after the flourishment of Hindu religion the people began to witness the introduction of various types of religious festivals including the different forms of dance. Indeed, these religious festivals also have played a major role in the enrichment of the cultural identity of the people. However the radicalist section has made an attempt to look it from a totally different angle. According to them the introduction of these festivals brought a serious effect to the normal economic life of the general people. Naoria Phullo took the leading role in this area of analysis. He started his observation from the introduction of *Ras Leela* a kind of religious dance form which was introduced during the reign of king Bheigyachandra. The introduction of this dance form is closely related with the introduction of *Vaisnavism* in the state. There are three types of *Ras Leela* dance i.e. *Basanta Ras*, *Maha Ras* and *Kunja Ras*. It is said that these three forms of dance was composed by king Bheigyachanda himself. The observation of Naoria Phullo was based on manner of spending time, energy and money by the common people in the name of religion. His ultimate idea was that the religious concept and idea of this dance form did not give any contribution to the developmental philosophy of the state rather its inner philosophy clearly reflected the idea of love making concept in the name of religion[20]. He further said that just after the end of the dance festival the actors and actresses specially the boy and the girl who played the role of Krishna and Radha did not pay much attention to their education and other duties. Such type of atmosphere affects to the growth of a new culture on education which is the basic need in the process of the establishment of meaningful society. This type of unhealthy situation, according to Phullo, is a good indication for the backwardness in the field of education in the state.[21] The hangover of the enjoyment of the *Ras Leela* dance was continued for quite long time particularly among the members of the families of the participants. As an impact of this hangover the members of these families continued the festive mood without giving much importance to the day today life of the household duties.[22] On the other side the result of the overspending money against their actual position of income and ignorance and negligence to the developmental work of the family also reached to their places without delay. The immediate impact, according to Phullo was the involvement in the unlawful activities in the society. He said that due to the failure to meet the immediate requirement sometimes the individual members of the family were compelled by this condition to indulge in some kind of illegal activities. As a result of this, sometimes they also received punishment from the administration. Naoria Phullo said that such type of unnatural development was the fruit of the establishment of *Ras Leela* dance by the members of this families.[22]

Naoria Phullo further said that *Ras Leela Dance* was not the end of the religious festival introduced by the Brahmins in Manipur. When the lean season was overed the Meitei Hindu people again established another religious festival called *Rakhal.* It is locally known as *Sansenba.* In this religious festival also almost all the participants were of teen age group. It is also a kind of dance drama and normally it was being played for two days. To make it a successful festival the arrangement and preparation took two or three month's time. Since it was strongly supported by the parents and guardians the children who participated in the dance drama they did not pay much attention in the programme of general schooling. Ultimately it gave serious disturbances in the normal working of general education of the children. On the other hand the establishment of this festival also involved a huge amount of money as expenditure.

Thus like *Ras Leela Dance* festival the *Rakhal* (Sansenba) dance drama also consumed time, energy and money. Besides, this dance drama also gave a serious impact in the environment of the surrounding areas. According to the observation of Naoria Phullo such type of unhealthy social atmosphere did not make any room to understand the scene of fast changing activities of other neighbouring areas. He said that the activities of these festivals blocked the knowledge, energy and spirit of the Meitei people. In his observation he always expressed his deep concern about the boys and girls who would be the pillars of the next generation. He further said that let the money be spent but the only question was the disturbances given by these festivals to the younger generation people in the process of their movement for the attainment of new knowledge through proper education. On the basis of these observations he wanted to know the individual person or group of people who were ready to take the responsibilities for the losing of their precious time and energy due to the lack of proper attention in their educational carreer.[24]

Another religious festival is the birth day of Lord Krishna. It is popularly known as *Krishna Janma* or *Janmasthami* etc. On this very day the devotees of Lord Krishna went to the temples to worship the god. According to the religious practice all the devotees took fast on this very day. The inner concept was that if they observed fasting they would be able to fulfill their desire both in this world and other to come.

But Naoria Phullo made his observation about this religious festival totally from a different angle. His argument was based on the social life of the young people. He said that this type of religious festival did not make any room for the improvement of their knowledge for the development of the society rather it taught the youngster of this country of how to enter into the family way through the religious practices. The nature of enjoyment of this festival provides a very good room for the establishment of love relationship between the boys and girls and learned the art of marriage.[25] This practice is called in the local term as *Yumballon* (Art of family way). Indeed his observation was from the moral point of view in the social life of the people. In this connection he pointed out the nature of enjoyment in the name of the religion. The celebration of this religious festival was started right from the early hour of the morning on this particular day. In the early morning the devotees including the boys and girls went to the temples to worship the god. Then as a part of the festival the boys and girls in group went to the selected places like lakes and secluded areas to enjoy the birth of Lord Krishna. Such type of enjoyment was known among the youths as *Thamchet Chaba* (Eating of a kind of water fruit). Then in the evening the boys and girls played a kind of indoor game known as *Likkol.* This type of game is popularly known as *Likkol Sanaba* (to play Likkol). The arrangement of this game was made in a highly fashionable way. But the most interesting nature of this game was that both boys and girls have played the whole night. Even the parents were enjoying the game played by their daughters by sitting together with the unknown boys. Naoria Phullo said such type of indoor game which was encouraged by the society in the name of religion have contributed a good room for the development of undesirable elements on the morals of the youths of the country. He further said that this festival creates a platform for enjoying youthful days for the establishment of new family.

Naoria Phullo also gave a critical observation of the nature of the observance of *Durga Puja* festival purely from the heavy expenditure side of the people. No doubt for Hindu people it is a great religious festival. According to Phullo there was a sharp difference in the nature of the worshipping of *Goddess Durga* between Bengal which is considered as the original place of the worship of *Durga* and Manipur. He said in the case of Manipur it was a real festival. During these five days of religious function the people enjoyed various types of activities like dance, drama different types of song right from devotional to modern song etc. And it was organized inside the shed where the image of the goddess is worshiped. Thus the people enjoyed the festival by spending a lot of money. It was also made compulsory for every family to buy new clothes. But Phullo said that these new clothes were imported from the outside states and taking advantage of the situation the shopkeepers sold the clothes in very high rates. Whatever condition may be, the people purchased the new clothes under an impression that when goddess entered in the residence they should welcomed her with new clothes. He was of the view that such type impression was deliberately created by the religious people gave a lot of problems particularly to the poorer section of the society. On the other side this compulsory type practice was not done in any other places. Even the nature of celebration of *Goddess Durga* worshipping was also quite contradictory with the nature of other states.

Another Hindu religious festival was *Doljatra.* Local people called it *Yoaosang Kummei.* This festival is held every year in the month of March. The celebration of this festival is directly connected with the religious philosophy of Vaisnavism of Gouranga cult of Bengal. But Naoria Phullo's observation about the festival was not from the ideas of religious philosophy. Rather his argument about this festival was based on the nature of its observation. Indeed, the whole activities of this festival may be divided into three parts *i.e.* Pre Yaosang activities, Yaosang activities, and Post Yaosang activities. The pre Yaosang activities were carried out by the young boys with a unique religious concept called *Yaosang Koiba.* During this time young boys in group basis had gathered at selected places of their area and arranged some kind of feast with the vegetables which they have collected from different house without the knowledge of the household owners. Such type of collection of vegetables from the homestead of other people was known as *Yaosang Huranba* in the local language. Since this type of activities was carried on in the name of religion the people also enjoyed it. The Yaosang festival is observed for five days and it starts with the burning of a 'hut' (*Yoasang*) constructed mainly for this purpose. Then it is followed by the donation of money by the small children from every houses. This is called locally *Naka Thengba.* This practice is continued for two times i.e. evening of the first day and morning of the second day. It was followed by the colour festivals which were enjoyed by everybody irrespective of ages. Another part of the activities of this festival is to cllect money by the girls from the male passersby. Locally it is known as *Peisha Munba* (to take money). Then in the evening another item called *Thabal*

Chongba, a kind of folk dance which was performed by both girls and boys. This type of dance was continued even after the end of *Yaosang Festival.* Naoria Phullo gave a strong reservation on the style of the observation of this religious festival in the name of god. The stealing of vegetables for eating and woods for burning fire by the youths from the houses gave a very good education of the art of thief to the young boys who was supposed to take the leadership of next generation of the country.[26] He further said that once a young boy have indulged in any type of illegal action like robbery, theft etc. even in a small degree then they would continue the same action in a large scale way when they reached to a certain age. Definitely it would create a social problem in the state. He also mentioned the contradictory nature of observance of *Doljatra* festival between Manipur and other states in India. It is true that in other states this festival is observed only for one day whereas in the state of Manipur it is observed for five days. During these five days the people enjoyed the festival and spend their time by doing various type of activities. Thus during this period people did not give any attention for any type of positive work either for the country or for him or herself. From this point of view, Naoria Phullo observed that such type of religious festival did not give any contribution to the growth of the knowledge of the people. Rather it created a habit of how to spend the time in a festive mood. He further said that the worship of Hari, another name of God which is associated with the *Yaosang* festival (doljatra) in Manipur have contributed in the process of the removal of both wealth and knowledge from the possession of the indigenous people of Manipur.[27]

Apart from this the people also witnessed the introduction of different types of religious festivals. The *Meragi Niyom Lairik Taba* was one of them. This religious programme was held normally in the month of *Mera* (September and October). Indeed it was a kind of very good religious activities where the elderly and interested people of different age group could be involved. Under this religious practice most of the elderly people could hear the philosophy and ideas of Hindu religion from a person who was well versed in this subject. So this religious function was organized by the interested elderly people at a particular place. Practically this religious activity was continued for about one month without any break. The inner idea behind this religious function was to redeem the sin which was committed by the people during the time of cultivation. It was believed that during the time of cultivation people gave torture to the animals which were used to plough agricultural land.[28] Thus in order to get themselves free from the sin they organized this religious festival. During this time no people were allowed to do any kind of manual works. However if a close observation is to be made it can be suggested that Naoria Phullo was not against the religious philosophy behind it. But he was very particular about the nature and undisclosed motive of the introduction of this religious festival. He was of the view that this practice also rendered a good help in the continuous process of the exploitation in the weak economic life of the general people. After giving a good picture of the involvement of money in this religious function he strongly asserted that this system which was introduced by Hindu colonisers forced the general people to spend the money in the name of religion.[29] He was of the view that at that particular period of time the common people of Manipur, compared with their annual income the expenditure side in the name of so many religious festival was so high. Therefore people got a lot of suffesings from the heavy expenditure. But mainly because of their strong conviction in the practices of Hindu religion they were not able to see the real picture behind these religious practices which was introduced by the Brahmins deliberately.

The *Manglati* was another religious festival introduced by the Brahmins in this state. The rubbing of the outer floor of the temple in the early morning and to sing the devotional songs were the main features of this festival. The religious idea created by the Hindu colonizers was that if the people, particularly youths performed the work of rubbing the floor of the temple would go direct to the heavenly abode after their death. This was also another impression created by the religious people that the person who was able to reach the temple first and sing the devotee song the soul of the person would be able to go direct to the grove of *Brindavan* where the Hindu people strongly believed that the Lord Krishna and his fiancée Radha played dance the whole night. It was also believed that if the people performed all the requisite items of this festival after death they would be able to reborn as a human being with all qualifications of a great person. Because of this belief most of the people particularly boys and girls took a special attention to this religious festival. But according to Naoria Phullo this idea was deliberately created by the Brahmins in order to make themselves including their family members, free from the cold condition of winter season. Therefore they introduced this idea to meet double purposes. According to his observation the first purpose was to take the help of other people in the service of temple which was the basic duty of the family of the Brahmins and secondly by doing so all the members of the were free from doing the service of temple. So he said that such type of policy which was deliberately adopted with a basic motive for their benefit was accepted by the foolish Meitei people as a very important religious festival. With this observation he further said that the only benefit which was acquired by the people from the worshipping of Krishna was to earn knowledge of how they would become a poor person.[31]

Ignorance to the General Education

Apart from these critical general observation on the nature and practices of the religious festivals Naoria Phullo also had pointed out a serious view of a negative impact produced by these religious activities on education and language. According to his argument the Hinduisation activities under the Brahmins had rendered a great contribution in the process of sharp declining of the importance of Manipuri language in the mindset of the people. It was mainly because of their strong attachment to the new religion, an impression was developed among the people that to know the Sanskrit or Bengali language and to learn the devotional songs of Hindu religion was more beneficial than to go to general education. The common people began to believe that the general education system was a useless exercise. Because of this different outlook to the system of general education the people paid much attention to the type of education related with the practice of Hindu religion. Accordingly they always tried to send their children to the teachers who were well verse in the art of devotional song of new religion. He also said that the attempt of the parents was also encouraged by these teachers. They created an impression among the people that to go to school for general education was not an act of obedience. Rather it would lay a foundation for the growth of the idea of the lack of discipline among the children. Therefore they asked the guardians to encourage their children in the system of education of salutation to the God and Goddesses.[32]

Thus due to the lack of strong initiative from the guardians to the knowledge of general education the boys and girls of this place had little information about the ongoing trend in the social, political and even the economic scenario of the surrounding areas outside Manipur. Ultimately the youths of this place were not able to get any type of opportunity to come out or even to prepare for any type of competition in the race of the developmental process which was going on in other areas. In this respect Naoria Phullo was of the view that the growth of economic hardship both to the family and society was the immediate impact of the ignorance of the system of the acquisition of new knowledge. Such type of hardship which was faced by the innocent people, according to his observation, was mainly due to the unhealthy religious policy of the Brahmins. He further said that those religious colonizers had misled the people in the wrong path. It was mainly because of their strong influence the parents had developed an impression that to learn devotional songs would get more respect from the society rather than to go to school for general education. They thought that if their children were able to master in the art of music and songs which was related with the Hindu religion they would be able to earn maximum recognition from the society. This was also the common notion among the general people that general education system did not make any room for the posterity of the family. Naoria Phullo further said that in the area of Hinduism there was no place for knowledgeable persons. Rather their ideas and practices had squeezed the knowledge and growing level of the degree of intellect of the Meitei people. On the basis of this observation he further said that due to their full attention and initiative to the dance, music and other religious festivals they did not have the time to spare some moments to think for the development of the society. Ultimately such conditions laid a basic foundation for having a downward trend in the economic life of the state. The problem of the financial crisis became a serious issue of every family. And ultimately it produced a sever type of question even to the very existence of the distinctive identity of the people of this state. Naoria Phullo said that such type of policy of the Brahmins was nothing but to create a space for the establishment of a den so called 'poor' in every Meitei family of this state.[33] Another impression which was developed in the minds of the people was that to go to school for English education was an act of untouchable. Therefore it is also mentioned that in an unavoidable circumstances the parents always put the school dresses separately. They refused to mix up the school dresses with other dresses because they considered it as an unclean article. Their children were not allowed to enter inside the house with school dress and so before entering they changed a new clothe. Because of this situation most of the parents did not send their children for English education. Therefore they have given more emphasis in the learning of devotional songs and music. Naoria Phullo observed that such type of the growth of unhealthy type of ideas among the parents had created a sever confusion in the nature of the thinking process of the people as whole. The ironical part of the Meitei Hindu people as remarked by Phullo was that on one side these people always considered the English education system as untouchable because it was introduced by the people coming from other areas, Whereas on the other side again these people always took all the Hindu religious books written by the '*Mayangs*' (outsider) was considered as sacred books. He further mentioned another self contradictory nature on the part of the Meitei Hindu people. He said these people they took English people and their education system as an untouchable one. On the other hand these people again paid a high respect to those *Mayangs* who received the modern English education either in India or Britain. Such type of self-contradictory nature in their approach has produced a confusing situation in the whole mindset of the Manipuri society. The elderly people always thought that to learn religious song and music was the best form of education which can give opportunity to earn their livelihood. Even the mothers nurtured their children with the hope that in future their children would become a great singer of devotional song of Hindu religion. It is also said that even in the marriage market a youth having a good knowledge of singing and art of other type of music have got a better prospect than others. Naoria Phullo said such type of notion was deliberately planted by the Brahmins in order to curb the possibilities of the growth of new ideas and scientific outlook and degree of intellect among the future generation people of the society. Thus due to the social ostracism practices the people did not pay much attention for the growth of modern education system in the state. Ultimately it brought a drastic effect in the process to the growth of new ideas among the people.

On the other hand all the youths were confined their energy and time in the religious ideas and devotional songs which were popularly known as the '*Hari Sankirtan,*' Because of this new social phenomena the people particularly the youths were not able to pay any type of positive attention to the issues which was related with the developmental items of the state and society. It is mentioned that at that particular time the '*Hari Sankirtan*' was considered by the Meitei Hindu people as a very important religious item. Therefore they always paid respect to those persons who regularly attended this religious song as a pious person. Naoria Phullo said this religious item could be well organized even by the uneducated peoples. It did not require any type of service from the educated and knowledgeable persons. Even a foolish person who was able to sing religious song could be a member of the 'Hari Sankirtan'[34]. He further said that since the Meitei Hindu people learned the religious songs and hymns etc mostly from the Bengali language they performed all religious activities including Sankirtan in this language. But the person who was well verse in the Bengali song did not know the meaning of the words. On the other hand most of the religious theme of the Sankirtan was on the personal relationship between either Krishna and Radha or Gouranga and Bishnupriya. Therefore, according to Phullo, there were so many words which ought not to be mentioned even in the public. He also mentioned that when Bangali audiences heard all such type of derogatory words as a part of the body of the song they turned their faces and ultimately came out from the places where the Sankirtan function was organized. On the basis of this observation Phullo said that to make room for the dispel of audience was the beauty and important quality of the sankirtan of the Meitei Hindu people.[35] But only the irony part which was mentioned by Phullo was that still people paid high respect to those singers who did not know anything about the meaning of the songs and hymns. So according to his opinion these tragedies were the creation of the influence of the Brahmin people in Manipur.

But it is very interesting to note that in his severe criticism to the nature of the Hindu way of religious practices Phullo never attack the religious philosophy and concept of the Hinduism. From this evidences it can be suggested that perhaps his only concerned was the undesirable religious practices which was introduced by the Brahmins in the state. He always thought that the Brahmins, by using the tools of religion, deliberately tried to destroy the economic strength of the people of Manipur. This idea was clearly reflected in his writing and arguments. On the basis of this observation he said that the Meitei people were now in the world of a big dream. Due to this condition they were not able to know anything about the development which was existed in the surrounding areas. They did not know when and how they could open their eyes and they also did not know how they would be able to come out from the den of hypnotism of the Brahmins He further said that when the people of other countries made a serious successful attempt for the growth and development of their areas the Meitei people still enjoy their life in a dream of happiness. The dreams as pointed out by Phullo were:-

- To accept Mayang (outsiders) religion as their religion.
- To accept the places Mayang Gurus as their sacred religious places.

- To accept the traditional religious deity as untouchable one and to admit the Mayang diety as pure god.
- To change the land of Meitei, which regarded by the forefathers as an areas of sacred religious place as the land of demon.
- To make the indigenous language as untouchable and Mayang language as pure.
- To accept Mayang songs as their songs.
- To admit the books written in Mayang language and script as the books of Meitei.
- To admit the history of the forefathers of Mayang as the history of Meities.[36]

With this contradictory misconception the Meitei people considered themselves as a separate group of people. He also asserted that the Meitei people under the influence of the hypnotism of the Brahmins.

He also said that the introduction of excessive degree of religious festivals has created a serious effect in the process of the growth and development of the country. This festival brought a serious condition for the growth of the deteriorating atmosphere in the courage, intellectual and property of the indigenous people of this place. He further observed that whatever the value of the quantity of their annual income was transferred into the hands of the Brahmins through the channel of religious practices and other types of festival. In addition to this, it is further mentioned that the Brahmins had reached their hands even to the fruits and vegetables which were grew into the homestead of the people. It was made an obligatory for every family that the first bear fruit or vegetable of the plant in their home should be brought to the Hindu deity. The Brahmins had created an impression in the minds of the people that if the members of the family did not follow this practice a bad effect would come to the family. With this observation Naoria Phullo said that on the basis of this belief the people sacrificed whatever they had in their purse and automatically the goddess of food grains of the indigenous people have entered into the granary of the Mayangs and this was the product of the creation of the Brahmins.

With this observation he further said that to change the dress of religious belief was the only way to the development and prosperity of the Meitei people[37]. Therefore he asked the people to prepare for a new dress of religion. Actually he was not in favour of the destruction of the principles of the Hindu religion. His only objective was to replace the religious dress of the Hindu religion by the indigenous religion of this place. He strongly asserted that the parasites became the master and the real master is now inside the unbreakable jail of the victim of new religion. Accordingly he made a strong appeal to all the people not to accept the influence of Brahmins whom were considered by Phullo as parasite. He also asked the people to remove all the dirty Hindu religious influence from their mindset. Apart from this he also asked the people to respect the sacred religious places of their forefathers. He further said that if the indigenous people did not prepare to remove the influence of cargo cult and if they continue to depend all their social life to the *Mayangs* they would not be able to see their real identity. On the background of these arguments he also made an appeal to all the people to encourage the Manipuri language so that it would rendera great help in the process of the strengthening of the distinctive identity of the Manipuri people. At the same time he also made an appeal to all the people to maintain their unity in order to protect themselves from any type undesirable disturbances which affect the integrity and solidarity of the country.

He was also of the view that whatever the activities of any type either on social or religion which was done by the people was based on the platform of a dream world. The people spend money in the festivals of the dream world. Therefore he strongly asserted that "if we continue our religious life by depending to the religious principles and practices of *Mayang* people all our income whatever earned annually would be completely exhausted."[38] He also expressed his apprehension to the exiting ongoing condition of the people. He said if the people continued further the existing social and religious practices under the influence of the new religion the Meitei people would not be able to participate in the race of the competition with the people of other countries. The whole financial discipline of the people and country would be seriously affected and automatically it would effect the day to day life of the people. He further said that if the people were not able to get a square meal effectively the concept of education which gives the only source for the growth of humane resource would become meaningless. He had categorically pointed out that so long as the Meitei people continue the inferiority complex to the Mayangs they would not be able to get or to maintain the self sufficiency of economy. He also lamented that the parasitic attitude of the people were so strong that they always considered all the books written by *Mayangs* in their language as their own books. So he strongly emphasized for the encouragement of Manipuri language. However he was fully convinced that all these problems and sufferings faced by the people was mainly due to the Hindu religious practices and festivals introduced by the Hindu religious colonisers. He strongly felt that all these problems would be overcome only when the people changed their religious dress from Hinduism to the indigenous religion.

On the solid foundation of this ideological principle Naoria Phullo had prepared to launch a mass movement for the revitalization of the indigenous religious concept and practices. He was also fully aware that a successful movement could be done only when there was a platform which can be used as a safety valve for future action. He also expressed his unhappiness to see the deteriorating condition of the people. He was of the view that when they opened their eyes after a long sleep they found that nothing was left for the people of Manipur. Everything was in the hands of the outsiders. With these firm conviction on religious ideology and for the promotion of the distinctive identity of the Manipuri people Naoria Phullo started a mass campaign for the revitalization of the primary religion of this country and for the establishment of a social identity of the people from the platform of 'Apokpa Marup'. Therefore the establishment of this social and religious organization was indeed a watershed in the entire history of this country because it laid a formidable basic foundation for the growth of the expansion of anti-Hindu stand among the people of Manipur. On the other hand it makes room for the development of the idea for having a separate social identity in their own political system.

NOTES

1. Sairem Nilbir, *Lainingthou Sanamahi Amasung Sanamahi Laining Hingat Ihou,* 2002, p.114.
2. *Ibid.*
3. *Ibid.*, p.115.
4. *Ibid.*,
5. Naoria Phullo, *Eigi Wareng,* 1985, p.19.
6. *Ibid.*
7. *Ibid.*
8. *Ibid.*
9. *Ibid.*, p.22.
10. *Ibid.*, p.26.
11. *Ibid.*, p.26.
12. Sunder Moirangthem Sakok lamlen p. 7. Khuraijam Kumar..
13. B. Kullachandra Sharma is the informant of the writer.
14. Naoria Phullo, *op. cit.*, p.25.
15. *Ibid.*, p.27.
16. *Ibid.*, p.27.
17. *Ibid.*, p.28.
18. *Ibid.*, p.32.
19. *Ibid.*, p.30.
20. *Ibid.*, p.58.
21. *Ibid.*
22. Ibid., p. 59.
23. *Ibid.*
24. *Ibid.*, p.60.
25. *Ibid.*, p.61.
26. *Ibid.*, p.77.
27. *Ibid.*, p. 79.

28. *Ibid.*, p.65.
29. An open shed where the people assembled for religious songs and hymns.
30. Naoria Phullo, *op. cit.*, p.66.
31. *Ibid.*, p.67.
32. *Ibid.*, p.41.
33. *Ibid.*, p.46
34. *Ibid.*, p.52
35. *Ibid.*, p.53.
36. *Ibid.*, pp.89 – 90.
37. *Ibid.*, p.141.
38. *Ibid.*, p.143.

5

Meetei Marup and Brahma Sabha

The religious activities of Naoria Phullo to revitalize the concept and practices of the primary religion were warmly received in Manipur. The radical section of the society of this place considered it as a new phenomenon so also a significant development in the process of making an attempt to maintain the distinctive cultural and religious identity of the people. They thought that through this movement the people of Manipur would be able to free themselves from the social ostracism policy introduced by Brahma Sabha, the highest apex body of the Brahmins of Manipur. Under this policy the Brahmins had enjoyed to exercise their authoritative character over the common people in the name of religion. On the other hand, the people though fully aware of the injustices committed by this body, were not able to raise their voice against it because the activities of Brahma Sabha were carried on with a strong patronage of the king. So under their heinous religious policy the people of this place faced a lot of unbearable harassment for quit long time without giving any sign of protest. Rather they were waiting for an opportune time to make themselves free from the clutches of the outcaste policy of Brahma Sabha.

It is said that the news of the heroic effort of Naoria Phullo for the promotion of the idea and practices of the primary religion was brought to Manipur by Pukhrambam Surchand and his brother Pukhrambam Ibomcha. Both of them were goldsmith by profession. It is mentioned that five years just after the establishment of *Apopka Marup* they went to Cachar for some works. They stayed there for a considerable period of days. While they were in Cachar they had got an opportunity to meet Naoria Phullo. From him they were able to get a strong inspiration to work for the revitalization of the primary religion of Manipur. Apart from this they were able to get a good knowledge about the philosophical ideas of the primary religion from Phullo.[1] After coming back from Cachar they went to the house of their brother-in-law Takhellambam Bokul at Keishampat, Imphal and they narrated the whole story about their meeting with Naoria Phullo. It seems that Bokul was already a disgusted man to see the nature of present religious practices. So the moment he received the information he expressed his readiness to work for the promotion of primary religion. Thus they had prepared to work for giving awareness about the importance of the primary religion in the process of the protection of their identity. It is also mentioned that the news of the religious activities of *Apokpa Marup* reached in Manipur in the year 1934. It is said that one Takhellambam Bokul got this information from a person of their locality who had recently visited Cachar for his work.[2] Another version was that the news of the religious activities of Naoria Phullo reached to Takhellambam Bokul from one Motum Jamini Singh.[3] To him it was a great news and he also thought that it would give a great help in their attempt to give awareness to the common people about the existing scenario of the conflicting religious situation in the state. He took it as an opportune time for all the people who were in favour of the radical change in the religious life and for the promotion and preservation of the distinctive identity of the character of the primary religion of this place. So without giving any room for second thought he went to Cachar in 1935 on the day of the 'Janmaasthmi', along with Pukhrambam Surchand and Pukhrambam Ibomcha[4] to meet Naoria Phullo. In Cachar they lived in the house of one Ashem Tombi for about one and half years. During this period they met Naoria Phullo and from him they were able to get a fresh idea about the religious concept and nature of practices of the primary religion. They always considered this effort as a big stride towards the growth of the idea for the revitalization of the primary religion of this area. This type of new development also laid a good foundation for growth of several organizations among the people on the line of *Apokpa Marup*.

As already mentioned, the nature and degree of atrocities which was carried on in Manipur by the Brahma Sabha in the name of religion and also about their organization which was carried out under the strong patronage of the king is made clear. So under these existing circumstances the common people were not able to express their unhappiness openly against the excessive nature of this religious body. Thus taking the advantageous position of the strong support of the king and by adopting the policy of social ostracism of 'Mangba and Sengba'(clean and unclean) the members of the Brahma Sabha, had successfully hammered the growing wisdom and intellectual power of the people. The common people were forced to live under the carpet of the policy of religious atrocities of this organization. Therefore, although they had a strong tendency to give awareness to the common people about the religious development, the existing situation compelled them to move in a very slow pace. So until the outbreak of Second World War in the year 1939 they remained silent without doing any type of outward activities. In the meantime they had closely monitored the mindset of the common people. Indeed the period of nineteen forties was a very significant period in the history of the liberation movement of the people of India. The idea of anti colonialism and anti feudalism reached its zenith in the mindset of the people. Therefore they fought vehemently to make themselves S free from the colonial and feudal rule. The wave of this idea also reached to the people of Manipur particularly among the educated youths. This feeling was clearly evidenced by the issue for the establishment of responsible government in Manipur by the Nikhil Manipur Mahasabha in the year 1938. The demand to establish the responsible government means to abolish feudal and colonial system of administration. The growth of the feeling of anti-monarchical system clearly shows that the people were not happy with the authoritative rule of the king. The strong demand to abolish the system like 'Chandan Senkhai'[5],'Napet Senkhai'[6] and other types of social evil practices clearly indicated that the people were not happy with the social ostracism policy of the Mahasabha. People always thought that the religious policy of Brahma Sabha was the key factor for the growth of unhealthy atmosphere in the harmonious relationship in the social life of the people of Manipur. The radical section of the society considered this new phenomenon as an opportune time for them to give an awareness campaign for the revitalization of the concept and practices of the primary religion. The spontaneous outbreak of great women agitation in the year 1939 on the basic foundation of anti feudal and anti colonial also marked the beginning of explosive stage of the unhappiness of the people. It is also observed that the outbreak of the Great War further strengthened their stand and ultimately they began to express openly against the authoritative rule of the king and social discriminatory policy of the Brahma Sabha. The growth of such type of situation was considered by these people as an opportune moment to start the work very effectively. With this objective they began to break the ice and prepared for a big movement for the promotion and preservation of the religious and cultural identity of this place.

The outbreak of World War II and its resultant impact in Manipur in the year 1942 was a turning point particularly to Pukhrambam Surchand and his younger brother Ibomcha. It is said that when the cloud of the danger of war reached in Manipur they had shifted to the Thambalkhong village at Wangkhei area and stayed in the house one Lukram Anganghal. From there they had started to spread the philosophy and concept of the primary religion of this place by meeting to each and every person.[7] Thus with this small step they began to prepare for a long journey to revitalize the primary religion of Manipur. It is said that before the official declaration of the existence of *Meetei Marup* as a religious organization a small committee was formed consisting of seven members to prepare a ground work for having a platform for the religious movement. Their names were: - 1.Takhellambam Bokul, 2.Pukhrambam Surchand, 3. Pukhrambam

Ibomcha, 4.Angom Nungshirei, 5.Angom Lila Singh, and 6.Toijam Yaima.[8] People began to look upon such type of unprecedented development with great amazement and fear. At that time the general impression of the people was that to stand against the king and religious authoritative position of the Brahma Sabha as a crime. Therefore people had an impression that these people who prepared to defy the principles and practices of the state religion would get severe punishment from the authority. So to save themselves from the possible danger they always tried to avoid from those people who strongly advocated for the revitalization of primary religion. They even refused to mix up with in any social gathering. Such type of apprehensive character of the general people was indeed, a moving force to pro revitalization elements of the society for having a strong determination to give an uncompromising challenge to the existing norms and practices of Hinduism and undesirable social discriminatory policy of Brahma Sabha. Therefore finally they had decided to take an oath for giving a steep opposition to the authoritarian nature of the Brahma Sabha. The oath taking function was arranged with a lunch. They called it '*Wasak Chak Chanaba*'(to eat oath feast).[9] Such type of stand may be regarded as a big jump towards the achieving of their goal.

The 2nd September of 1944, the full moon day of the month of Langban (August/September), was a red letter day in the history of the religious revitalization movement in Manipur. On this very day a formal gathering was held by some selective persons at the residence of one Lukram Liklai at Thambalkhong. Their names were: - 1. Takhellambam Bokul, 2.Pukhrambam Surchand, 3. Pukhrambam Ibomcha, 4. Angom Nungshirei,5. Lukram Anganghal, 6.Toijam Yaima, 7.Wangkheimayum Modhusudon, 8. Sarangthem Angou, 9.Lukram Modhumangol, 10. Angom Yadov and 11. Hiyangthang Toni. But there is some confusion about the participation of Angom Nungshirei. It is said that out of fear he did not attend the meeting.[10] However, in other records his name was reflected in the list of participants in the gathering. In this meeting Bokul, Surchand and Ibomcha had narrated in detail about the nature of their meeting with Naoria Phullo. Finally they placed their views on the importance and immediate necessity for a serious effort to promote and foster the philosophy and practices of the primary religion which was enjoyed by the people of this country before the coming of Hinduism. Perhaps their view was mainly concerned with the preservation of the identity of the people. They thought that revitalization of the primary religion was the only answer to the question of the protection of the identity which was gradually eroded seriously just after the coming of Hinduism. The discussion was continued for quite long time. Thus after having a marathon discussion they all agreed to adopt certain resolutions in order to take a step to materialize their objective. Ultimately they all agreed to make a tireless effort to revitalize the content and practices of the primary religion which was closely associated with the life and identity with the people of this place from time immemorial.

Indeed, it was a significant step towards the achievement of their goal. They strongly asserted that the present religion and its practices were all foreign elements. At any rate it was not directly or indirectly connected with the history of the growth of the people of this place. Perhaps their argument was based on the universally accepted concept of cargo cult. They strongly emphasized that this foreign religion had spoiled the life and identity of the people of this place. On the basis of this firm conviction they had also started to work for the implementation of their objective by organizing the masses through certain religious norms and patterns. As a part of their programme and to strengthen their action they all agreed to meet on every sunday at the residence of Sarangthem Angou of Thambalkhong. Thus their sincere and dedicated efforts brought a new dimension in the religious outlook of the common people. Gradually people had started to judge the existing religious situation on basis of the assertion of these radical people. Whatever it may be, but it is also an undeniable fact that this new argument has produced a far reaching positive impact on the cultural and religious life of the people. From this fact it may be suggested that this small gathering, no doubt, was a step for the beginning for a gigantic mass involvement journey for making a new outlook in the religious and cultural life of the people of this state. Then as a part of the mass awareness program they had started to write and publish literatures on the concept and practices of the primary religion of this place. In the process they took a great help from the *'Puyas'(Ancient texts)* which was ignored for quite long time just after the coming of Hinduism. By taking information given by the *'Puyas'* they moved from one place to another to campaign for the revitalization of the traditional religion. They strongly asserted that their distinctive identity could be saved only through the maintenance of traditional religion. Therefore to give counter movements against the religious practices of the Hindu religion they had also agreed to open various fronts. The formation of *Ishei Pala* (singer group) was one of the most notable achievements of their attempt. Along with this they had also successfully prepared the religious rules and regulations to be practiced by the people from the time of the birth of a person till death. Thus the activity for the revitalization of primary religion was started with great enthusiasm.

Indeed, the formation of *Ishei Pala* (singer group) rendered a great help in the process of the strengthening of the movement. Through this platform they were able to spread the religious ideas and practices to the masses. The nature of the working of singer group was just like the Sankritan of the Hindu religion. The Meitei Hindu people always considered it as the most important part of the rites and rituals of the Hindu religion. Accordingly in their sitting on 30th April 1945 they had selected four ancient texts from which they prepared to write the poems for religious songs. The names of the books were:-1. *Lainingthou Laipao*, 2. *Thaina Nongin*, 3. *Echel* and 4. *Nonga Lambi.*[11] Lukram Iboton and Konjengbam Nabachandra were assigned to prepare songs from these books. Then they formed *Ishei Pala* (singer group) consisting of eighteen persons. Their names were:- 1. Lukram Iboton, Head drummer or *Hanjaba* 2.Konjengbam Nabachandra, *Ishei Hanba* (Head Singer) 3. Phurailatpam Sanahanbi ,*Hidang* 4. Nongthonbam Manao, *Seikhumba or Duhar*, 5. Pukhrambam Surchand, *Kholpangba* 6.Angom Nungshirei, *Mathang Kholpangba* 7.Toijam Yaima, 8.Achom Mani, 9.Pukhrambam Ibomcha,

10.Chongtham Gouro,*Duhar Mathang* 11.Sarangthem Thambalyaima, 12.Angom Lila Singh, 13.Aheibam Tombapu, 14.Lukram Modhumangol, 15Lukram Ibotombi, 16. Lairenmayum Yaima, 16. Lairenmaym Nityai and 18.Waikhom Kanhai.[12] It is recorded that when he was asked to become a member of the singer party Konjengbam Nabachandra was reluctant to accept the proposal out of the fear from the possible objection from his mother. Later on he also accepted the proposal of the leaders of the movement.[13] The same problem was also happened in the case of Lukram Iboton when he was asked to be a drummer of the singer party. Later on he also accepted the proposal. These facts clearly indicate the degree of the fear psychosis in the minds of the common people about the atrocities from the policy of social ostracism of Brahma Sabha. On the 23th May 1945 a large meeting was held at 2 p.m. at the residence of Pukhrambam Surchand under the presidentship of Takhenmaym Chaoba of Phougakchao Ithai. About one hundred and fifty persons from different villages were present. The meeting was opened with a devotional song and it was followed by an introductory speech from T. Bokul. In his opening remark he expressed his happiness and satisfaction to get the opportunity to use their mother tongue at the time of the worship of god and goddesses which was not in practice for quite a long time under the Hindu religion. He said that their main objective was not to change the basic philosophy of religion but to change the dress of the religious philosophy and practices of the '*Mayangs*'(foreigners).[14] He further said that the same character of the mythical heroes and heroines of the Hindu religion was also existed in the religious philosophy of the primary religion of the Manipuris. According to him the '*Mayang*' word '*Ishwar*' was of Manipuri word '*Ipuroi*'. Likewise the Hindu god *Vishnu,* which is believed as an invincible one was nothing but '*Sidaba Mapu*' of Manipuri. The nature of *Krishna,* who was believed by the Hindu religious people as the maker of universe was also existed in the traditional religion with a name called *Poklen Pokpa*, and Jaganath of Hindu religion may be equated with *Tengbanba Mapu* of primary religion.[15]

With this introductory speech the meeting started with a full of emotional and sentimental degree. After having a long deliberation the meeting unanimously adopted resolutions on various aspects. The framing of code of conduct which was to be followed by every person who accepted the nature of primary religion as their own religion was the most important noteworthy work of these activists. Accordingly they prepared a long list which contained almost all the issues related with cultural and religious life of the people. As a whole the meeting strongly emphasized to worship the deities of the pre Hindu period and to perform the rites and rituals through their own mother tongue. They also agreed to establish a platform through which the activities for the revitalization of their primary religion could be performed very effectively. They all agreed to call the name of this platform as *Meetei Marup Manipur State.*[16] The establishment of this religious organization was indeed, a great contributory outcome of this gathering. Apart from this they also accepted seven colours which represented the seven clans of the society as the official banner of this organization. Finally they all agreed to give up the religious practices of Hinduism and its way of life for all time. Thus after having a full preparation the establishment of Meetei Marup Manipur State was formally declared on the 14th May 1945.

The formal declaration of the establishment of the *Meetei Marup Manipur State* as the pole bearer for the growth of the idea of religious revitalization movement was arranged and prepared in a large scale way with great attention and utmost care. A religious feast was arranged and it was cooked by three persons. Their names were:-1.Gurumayum Bishesore, 2.Keisham Chaoba and 3.Pukhrambam Gokulchand. The active involvement and participation of a person from the Brahmin community in such anti Hindu movement itself may be treated as a noteworthy development in the process of their journey. One Sanasam Yaimachou of Kameng village was made the ceremonial master of the function. Then just after the ceremonial lunch was over they started the rituals with the devotional song presented by the members of the *Ishei Pala* (singing party). The theme of their song emphasized the contribution of mythical heroes and heroines who were believed to be the creator of the cosmos and living beings. In addition to this in their song they also praised the accountability of natural objects which were believed to have a close relationship with the human beings in their social and cultural life. After this Takhellambam Bokul gave a nice pen picture about the inner concept and philosophy of the primary religion which was once the only religion of the people before the coming of Hinduism. He also explained the reason why they wanted to remember their primary religion after a long gap of centuries. With this word he strongly asserted the immediate need to give up the Hindu religion and its way of life to maintain the national identity of the Manipuri people. Pukhrambam Surchand and his brother Ibomcha also expressed their happiness to get an opportunity to enjoy the previledge of using their mother tongue at the worship of god and in the performance of religious rites which was not accepted under the practices of Hindu religion. They also gave a detail picture of how the idea of Hinduism had entered into Manipur and they also explained the role of Shanti Das, the main religious preacher of Hinduism who compelled the people to embrace the new religion. Apart from this he also gave a very account of how he burnt down the important *Puyas* (ancient texts) with the knowledge of the king of Manipur. Thus these people who were in favour of a sharp radical change in the life of the people began to give a successful awareness campaign for the promotion of the primary religion of Manipur. Indeed this gathering marked a great landmark in the process for the religious revitalization movement in Manipur. It is mentioned that about one thousand people including women were present in the gathering. The name of the women who participated in the meeting were:- 1.Tongbram Ningol Sabi, Ningthem Pukhri Mapal, 2.Pukhrambam Ongbi Kamini, 3.Athokpam Ningol Yuboti, 4. Pukhrambam Ongbi Tampha, 5.Pukhrambam Ongbi Mukhi, 6. Sarangthem Ongbi Toleima, 7. Ngaseppam Ongbi Madhabi, 8. Konjengbam Ongbi Leibaklei, 9. Nongthongbam Ongbi Luwangleima, 10.Thokchom Ongbi Nungshirei, 11. Nongthongbam Ongbi Radhe, 12. Nongthongbam Ongbi Yuboti and 13. Laimayum Ongbi Mera.[17] Thus with the help of untiring endeavours these leaders were able to start a successful campaign for a religious revitalization movement in a most effective manner through the platform of *Meetei Marup.*

Ultimately it also produced a positive impact by giving a strong influence in the mindset of the common people. Now the people also began to think about the importance and immediate need for having a distinctive social and cultural identity based on their primary religion.

Such type of new trend of anti Hinduism phenomenon was a great concern to the Brahma Shabha, the highest apex body of the Hindu religion in Manipur. They took it as a serious threat to the very existence of the Hindu religion in this country so also the working of this body. On the other side they also began to come across the activities of anti Hindu character by some people who openly defied the nature of the practices of Hindu religion. They had started to remove the *chandan mark* of the Hindu religion and the number of sacred thread was also changed according to the norms of the primary religion. Thus because of the differences in the religious outlook a serious problem developed in the harmonious relationship among the people. To see the religious activities of the Meetei Marup some section of the people had a strong desire to check their growing strength and so they submitted an application to the Brahma Sabha against some leaders of the organization for their anti Hindu stand. The names of the applicant were; - 1.Laisangbam Tomba Singh 2.Longjam Tomchou Singh 3. Naorem Bokul Singh and 4. Leisangthem Keirungba Singh.[19] All of them was from Kameng village. In their application they said that the members of the *Meetei Marup* have stopped to put *chandan mark* on their forehead and the number of sacred thread was also reduced against the specific numbers of Hindu religion. As a whole they strongly emphasized the anti Hindu character of the members of the *Meetei Marup*. With these allegations they also expressed their apprehension to mix up with these people in any social gatherings. On the basis of this argument they made an appeal to the Brahma Sabha to give a final verdict according to the religious customary rule. As a response to their complain the Brahma Sabha through the official order vide Memo No. 1122 A.R.C. dated 8/6/45 of the Maharaja of Manipur, declared that those persons who did not put the *chandan mark* on their forehead and those persons who performed the rites and rituals of the death ceremony by the Manipuri language would be treated as an act of defiance of the existing religious practices of the state. This general order was issued on 10th June 1945.[20] But again on 12th June 1945 an official notice was served to the four leaders of the Meetei Marup to attend the royal court for their active involvement in the anti Hindu religious efforts. Their names were 1.Aheibam Tombapu, 2. Lairenmayum Nityai, 3.Konjengbam Nabachandra and 4.Sanjenbam Yaima Achaiba.[21] The official notice also asked the other people who embraced the practices of traditional religion to come to the royal court along with these four leaders. The leaders of the Meetei Marup and other people who practiced the primary religion always considered such type of repressive action of the royal court as a great challenge and so in order to sustain their activities they have prepared both physically and mentally to meet any type of undesirable action which might have been occurred against the line of their thinking. Therefore on this particular day also they went to the royal court under the leadership of Pukhrambam Surchand and Pukhrambam Ibomcha to give a big challenge against the members of Brahma Sabha. All the people put sacred thread of seven strings and *chandan* mark not on the system of Hindu religion. They also wear red cloths. However, perhaps out of fear from the possible danger Angom Nungshirei and Lukram Anganghal did not attend the royal court. But later on after getting all the information of the nature of discussion they also came to attend the court.[22] About two hundred people were assembled there. The debate between the members of Brahma Sabha and Meetei Marup was held in the royal durbar hall. Pukhrambam Surchand and Ibomcha placed all the historical facts about the culture and religion which was enjoyed by the people of this place before the coming of Hindu religion. So they strongly tried to justify their religious and cultural stand for having a distinctive identity of their own. The members of the Brahma Sabha who were present on that day were very much agitated to hear the position and stand of Meetei Marup. While the debate was going on Shri Kongrailakpam Lalhari Sharma, a member of Brahma Shabha immediately stood up from his sitting place and forcibly tried to brush out the chandan mark of

Konjengbam Nabachandra by his own hand which he put according to the belief of the primary religion.[23] He also asked Nabachandra to give explanation why he adopted anti-Hindu stand. The people who assembled there were not very happy to the unexpected and undesirable behavior of the respectable member of the Brahma Sabha. But out of respect of the dignity and sanctity of the royal palace they remained silent by not uttering even a single word against the behavior of the member. In their debate the leaders of the Meetei Marup strongly asserted that the basic objective of their organization was not to ignore or neglect god whatever it may be but their only stand was to worship god and perform the rites and rituals through their own language.[24] They had placed their view very categorically that they did not like to worship god through foreign language.

On 19th June 1945 the Brahma Sabha again asked some leaders of the Meetei Marup to attend the royal court. The name of the leaders who were listed to attend the court were;- 1. Pukhrambam Surchan,2.Pukhrambam Ibomcha, 3.Takhellambam Bokul, 4.Konjengbam Nabachandra, 5.Sanjenbam Yaimachouba, 6.Aheibam Tombapu, 7.Lairenmayum Nityai, 8. Wangkheimayum Tombiand 9. Gurumaym Bishesore etc.[25] The other members of the organization did not leave their leaders alone. This time also a large number of people went to the royal court to witness the debate. The meeting was started with an ugly and undesirable scene. At that time sitting arrangement was made only either on carpet or mattress. Like the other members of the Brahma Sabha the two leaders of the Marup Wangkheimayum Tombi and Gurumayum Bishesore also sat on the carpet by crossing the legs *(Khongrai chanba)*. Without having any direct relevance with the issue Shri Kongrailakpam Lalhari Sharma, a member of the Brahma Sabha, immediately reacted to the nature of the sitting style of the two persons as an act of the lack of respect to the august body. They also retorted that they simply follwed the sitting style of Sabha. They further asked the member to give the alternative sitting style. Lalhari Sharma was very much irritated to the answer and immediately asked the guards to throw them out from the meeting hall. Such type of illogical nature of the member of the Brahma

Sabha was highly condemned by the people who were assembled at the surrounding areas of the meeting place. Then the members of the Sabha began to put a volley of questions about nature and concept of the religion which was initiated by the members of the *Meetei Marup*. They also asked whether the Meeteis had their religious book like 'Vedas' of Hindu religion. The leaders gave a very long explanation about the concept and nature of practices about the worship of *Sanamahi* the supreme deity of the primary religion of the people of Manipur. They also claimed that these religious practices were just like the Vedas of Hindu. Thus for quite long time the religious debate was going on between the members of two religious groups. While the endless debate was going on one Laikhuram Ibungohal from the Wangkhei area made an appeal to the members of the Brahma Sabha not to give any type of restriction to the working of the Meetei Marup.[26] Thus the debate came to an end with a moral victory on the side of the leaders of the Meetei Marup.

While several attempts by the members of the Brahman Sabha for the suppression of the anti Hindu stand were going on the activities of the religious revitalization movement of the Meetei Marup was also continued with strong vigour and enthusiasm. After the formal declaration of the establishment of this religious and cultural organization the next meeting of the Marup was held at Soibam Leikai on 18th July 1945.[27] It is mentioned that this religious meeting was organised at the initiative of one Angom Natho and it was held at the mandop of one Brahmacharimayum Bapu Sharma. It is indeed a very interesting and noteworthy new phenomenon to understand how and why the anti Hindu religious meeting was permitted to organize at the temple place of Brahmin. Whatever the case may be, such type of new outlook may be taken as a big positive stride in favour of the sincere attempts of the members of the Meetei Marup. It is also mentioned that the nature of the arrangement and style of wording of the religious song was well received even by those persons who were the staunch believer of Hindu religion. It is also said that at the special request of one Rajkumar Birchandrasana the same religious song was again sung for second time. Then as a mark of respect

Birchandrasana presented gifts to all the members of the singer party. After this the activities of the awareness programme of the organization was continued without any gap. On 19th July 1945 another meeting was held at the residence of Khangembam Ibomcha of Sagolband area. In the meantime the members of the Meetei Marup got information that the Brahma Sabha would announce the verdict of the case on the 20th July 1945. On this very day a large number of people went to the royal court to hear the verdict of the case. When the people assembled near the court Shri Lalhari Sharma, a member of the Brahma Sabha asked the members of the Meetei Marup not to enter near the court as they were opposed to the deity Govinda and Hindu way of life. He also said that in future there would be no activities of Meetei Marup in Manipur and nobody would be allowed to use Manipuri language at the time of singing of religious song and performance of rites and rituals. He also warned the people that if anybody refused to obey the directive they would get royal punishment. He further said that if any person follow the religious practice of Meetei Marup they would get severe type of punishment according to the customary law of the country.[28] The people who were present there were not happy with the nature of the Brahmin chauvinistic character of Lalhari Sharma. Some people even said that it was not the verdict of the royal court but the personnel opinion of Lalhari Sharma. But such type of attempt to demoralize the growing spirit of the organization did not produce any negative impact in their efforts. Rather it rendered a great contribution to the process of the strengthening of their efforts to revitalize the primary religion of the people of Manipur. On this very day itself the members of the Meetei Marup performed their religious discussion at the residence of one Tensubam Lamphel of Top village.

However, in the process of their ongoing religious revitalization movement the leaders of the Meetei Marup also faced a number of hurdles and resistance from different quarters. In a particular incident the people of Thambalkhong made an attempt to expel Pukhrambam Surchand and his brother Ibomcha from their locality as they thought that their presence in their locality would create problem and it might be an act of inviting anger of the members of Brahma Sabha and king. They were of the view that their existence in their locality would face danger from the policy of social ostracism. Apart from this they also thought that if these people stayed together with them no other persons from other localities would come to their area to attend any type of social and religious function. When this was the unhealthy social environment in this locality one Toijam Muji Singh died and the family members had prepared for the performance of the death ceremony. However they were not able to do it very effectively because they had an apprehension that the people of other localities might be reluctant to attend the function. At that time most of the people did not like to see the presence of these anti Hindu people in any social and religious gathering. Therefore in order to get themselves free from the presence of these people in their locality some people at the initiative of Sarangthem Jugai, Sarangthem Amudon, Toijam Langonjaoba and Toijam Lukhoiba went to the palace to make an appeal to His Highness the Maharaja of Manipur against these people. They requested Maharaja Budhachandra to expel Pukhrambam Surchand and his brother Ibomcha from their locality as they had adopted an anti Hindu stand which was against principles of state religion. But Maharaj Budhachanra, who was the custodian of state religion, did not entertain their request. Rather he rebuked them for their attempt to interfere in the religious belief of other people. The name of the persons who went to the palace were:- 1. Toijam Langoljao, 2. Toijam Angou, 3. Toijam Itoba, 4. Toijam Amu, 5. Toijam Nene, 6. Toijam Ingoba, 7. Toijam Amon, 8. Toijam Angoutombi, 9. Toijam Muru, 10. Toijam Liklai, 11. Toijam Anou, 12. Sarangthem Amudomba, 13. Sarangthem Kammu, 14. Sarangthem Amudomba, 15. Sarangthem Amumacga, 16. Lukram Tompok, 17. Laishram Athoi, 18. Laishram Phejao, 19. Angou Bosan, 20. Sarangthem Chaoren, 21. Nahakpam Lamjenyangba etc.[29] Just after coming back from the defeated mission, they again made a serious attempt to expel Surchand and Ibomcha by using deathly weapons. They tried to give humiliation while they were working at their house. Meanwhile some leaders of the Meetei Marup like Sarangthem Natho,

Chongtham Gouro, Lukram Iboton, Toijam Yaima, Toijam Muhori, Maibam Kokngang, Nameirakpam Nilo etc. also reached the spot. Luckily with their efforts the situation was brought under control. Both Surchand and Ibomcha were not happy with the undesirable attitude of some people of their locality. So in order to bring a final solution they filed a case to the police. Immediately some police personnel along with Laishram Pakka Babu reached at the residence of Toijam Angoutombi and enquired the reason for their illegal action. The people who were involved in the case were not able to give proper justification of their action. They simply said that their attempt to expel Surchan and Ibomcha was mainly because of the possible danger from the social ostracism policy of the Brahma Sabha. Very categorically they stated that if they lived together with these anti Hindu people in the same locality they would get punishment from the Brahma Sabha. They also thought that if the two brothers lived in their locality the Brahma Sabha would declare their place as an unclean area. The police people took their action as a great crime and so they were asked to pay a fine of rupees one thousand. It is also mentioned that the money had to be collected from every houses who were involved in the attack. Further they were also asked by the police to tender their apology to Surchand and Ibomcha for their misconduct. The helpless people who committed the crime had no other alternative and some of them tendered their apology to them. It is also mentioned that since many people had refused to pay money for fine and having no alternative one Sarangthen Jugai had voluntured to pay all the money from his own pocket. After this incident the people of the whole area of Thambalkhong was divided into three groups. Such type of undesirable new phenomena in the harmonious relation of the people of that area was regarded by some people as the creation of the Brahma Sabha. On the other hand it is also observed that such type of reaction from the unexpected corner of the society also had rendered a great natural contribution to the process of the strengthening of their activities. With such great obstacles and hurdles the members of the Meetei Marup began to move forward with new vigour and spirit to achieve their ultimate objective.

Just after having a very good experience of the conflict and hurdles from the members of the Brahma Sabha the leaders of the Marup began to give more attention to the religious idea and philosophy of the primary religion which they were trying to foster very effectively. With this objective, as a first effort of their attempt Pukhrambam Surchand went to Cachar to collect all the relevant Puyas which were in the possession of Naoria Phullo. Thus with the help of these ancient texts the leaders of Meetei Marup were able to give awareness of the new religious ideas and concepts of the primary religion to the people. With this new venture the activities of the religious revitalization movement of the Meetei Marup was moving very fast in a positive direction throughout the length and breath of Manipur particularly in the valley areas. A series of religious meeting was organised in various places along with the members of the singer group. Their sincere efforts were widely well received by many people and some of them began to give up the Hindu religion and its way of life and began to embrace the idea of primary religion. But unfortunately while the momentum of the movement started to reach its peak Pukhrambam Surchand one of the founder leader of the Marup expired on1st March 1947.[27] His untimely death had produced two important mix impacts. On the one hand his sudden demised when the time the movement for religious revitalization was in full swing, was a serious irreparable loss of the whole organization but on the other side it also gave a new blood to the moral and spirit of the members of the Marup. Just after his death the religious activities of the organization began to come out openly without any fear and apprehension from any quarter of the society. It is recorded that the ritual of the death ceremony of late Surchand was performed at his place on 13th March 1947 under the religious belief of the *Marup*. All the members and well wishers had attend the ceremony by raising banner and shouting slogan in favour of the organization. Such type of militant character of the members of the organization was indeed the reaction of the negative attitude of the state and Brahma Sabha. It was an unprecedented development and a direct challenge to the hegemonistic and chauvinistic attitude of the members of the Mahasabha.

Then on 31st October 1947 under the official Memo No 61 the Brahma Sabha gave verdict of the case No.107/48[30] which was related with the religious activities of the Meetei Marup. The verdict of the court alleged thirty-eight persons for their active involvement in the anti-Hindu religious movement of Meetei Marup and also for embracing 'Sanamahi Religion'. They were also charged by the court for ignoring the Vedas the secret book of Hinduism and Brahmins and for adopting different type of religious life against the principles of Hinduism. On the basis of these arguments the court declared them as socially untouchable persons and the verdict further said that nobody should be allowed them to mix up in any social and religious functions and gatherings. The names of the persons were:

- Aheibam Tombapu Singh — Kameng Village.
- Lairenrn aym Nityai Singh — do
- Sanjenbam Yaimachouba Singh — do
- Konjengbam Nabachandra Singh — do
- Achom Goura Singh — do
- Thokchom Yadov Singh — do
- Nongthongbam Gourasingh Singh — do
- Noongthongbam Naran Singh — do
- Waikhom Kanhai Singh — do
- Waikhom Tomba Singh — do
- Aheibam Shamu Singh — do
- Mangsidam Tomba Singh — do
- Haobuijam Iboton Singh — Sega Lambi
- Yaima Nongsa — Thambalkhong
- Sarangthem Angou Singh — Wangkhei
- Atombapu Aheibam — Wangkhei

• Tensubam Lamphel Singh	Kongpan
• Gokulchand Thiyam	Wangkhei
• Tomba Laishram	Keishampat
• Ngaseppam Manickchand Singh	do
• Takhellambam Bokun Singh	do
• Pukhrambam Surchand Singh	Thambalkhong
• Pukhrambam Ibomcha Singh	do
• Lukram Iboton Singh	do
• Sarangthem Thambalyaima Singh	do
• Angom Lila Singh	do
• Lukram Ibotombi Singh	do
• Lukram Modhumangol Singh	do
• Ngangom Gouranga Singh	Sekta Village
• Yaikhom Khamba singh	do
• Yendrambam Chaoba Singh	do
• Wakambam Bokul Singh	Pungdongbam
• Irungbam Nongyai Singh	do
• Moiurangthem Choulidar Parijat Singh	Khudrakpam
• Naorem Amuleisang singh	do
• Nandeibam Iboton Singh	do
• Sanasam Mani Singh	do
• Moirangthem Bokun Singh	do.[31]

The nature of the verdict of the court was an expected result to all the members of the Meetei Marup. From the very beginning they knew that the verdict would be purely one sided. Therefore this result did not make any room for having some kind of set back to the spirit and moral of the members of the organization. Rather this new phenomenon gave a great courage to the members of the organization. So immediately just after getting the verdit they had prepared to give a quick response and reaction to the decision of the Brahma Sabha. As an answer to the allegation of the Brahma Sabha the leader of the organization wrote an open letter to the public in which they put several questions and queries to the members of the Brahma Sabha. Their strong argument was that how could it be possible to declare a person ostracized if they refused to speak the Mayang(foreign) language. So they asked the leaders of the Brahma Sabha to give a logical and rational answer to their question.[32] This hand out paper was signed by Pukhrambam Ibomcha. The Congress Party of Manipur also reacted very sharply to the verdict of the Brahma Sabha. In a press release signed by one Shamungou the Secretary of the party asked the state government not to support the decision of the Brahma Sabha. They said that since the Dominion Government of India had already emphasized for the establishment of secularism in the social life of the country the state government should not extend their administrative hand in any religious issue from their administrative position. Therefore they had requested the state government not to circulate the verdict of the Brahma Sabha.[33]

On the other hand, in spite of so many obstacles and hindrances, the religious activity of the organization was also continued further. As a part of their movement they had also constructed a temple (Phura) of six feet and eight feet size at a place called Chingoi[34] in the Nongmaiching hill popularly known as Baruni hill. The construction of temple was started from the 25th February 1948. But this temple was demolished at the directive of Maharaj Budhachandra. It is mentioned that Budhachandra went with some of his people at the top of the Baruni hill with an objective to construct the temple of God Mahadeva(Hindu God). After staying there for about two or three months he came back and on the way back he saw the temple constructed by the Meetei Marup. He asked the people about the owner of the temple. One Sapam Thoiba Singh of Moirang Kampu village disclosed the real owner of the temple. He said it was constructed by the members of the Meetei Marup to worship their traditional deity. After getting the reply from him Maharaja immediately asked them to demolish it and he further said that he was going to construct a temple and mandop very soon. It is also said that he took signature of Thoiba in a blank paper and the remaining wordings were written at the dictation of the Maharaja.[35] All the members of Meetei Marup who were at the spot were in a helpless position and accordingly they demolished the temple constructed by their own hands and went back with a heavy heart. Then after some days a group of people from Cachar Assam came to Manipur to perform the rites and rituals of their forefathers at the Chingoi River under their traditional religious belief and practices. When they reached the spot of the bank of the river they found that Maharaja Budhachandra was already stationed there. The people from Cachar were accompanied by Takhellambam Bokul, a leader of Meetei Marup and also a member of the Manipur Legislative Assembly. Immediately, when he saw the Maharaja, he along with some people went to his (Maharaja) place and requested him to give permission so that the people would be able to perform their religious rites and rituals. Maharaja asked them to do their religious rites to a place at some distance from his sitting area. The people were not happy to the undesirable nature and attitude of the Maharaja. And without uttering even a single word they began to disperse from that place. However at the special request from P. Ibomcha another leader of Meetei Marup the people performed their religious rites and rituals at a particular place of Chingoi River. This incident was known among the members of Meetei Marup as *Chingoi Wathok*(catastrophe of Chingoi). Thus in their attempt to revitalize the primary religion of Manipur the members and leaders had come across a lot of unexpected hurdles from the different corners of the society.

The attempt of the Brahma Sabha to discredit and destabilise the entire religious activities of the Meetei Marup was continued further. From their several attempts it is quite clear that their only objective was to demonstrate to the common people that there was no concept and philosophy of the primary religion of Manipur which the members of the Meetei Marup were trying to spread among the masses. With this sole objective again they again organized a religious debate on 28th May 1950 at Yumnam Leikai. The theme of the debate was 'Gouriya religion and religion of Meetei Marup'.[36] Officially this religious debate was organized in the name of one religious body called '*Yumnam Leikai Nityainanda Marup*'. The notice and invitation was issued and circulated by one Kalachan Singh as the secretary of this organization. The names of the persons who were going to participate from the side of the Brahma Sabha were:

- Kashiram Sharma Bidya Ratna
- Sibadatta Sharma Tarka, Tarka Tirtha
- Brajabihari Sharma Kyaiba, Smriti Biyakaran Tirtha.
- Lalhari Sharma Biyakaran Tirtha
- Nutunchandra Sharma Biyakaran Tirtha
- Brajamani Sharma
- Kalachand Singh Shastrit B.A.

It is also mentioned that one Ngaseppam Manikchand Singh was supposed to represent the Meetei Marup in this religious debate. Then some kind of confusion and misunderstanding cropped up among the leaders of the organization and finally after having a thorough discussion the organization decided to sent Pukhrambam Ibomcha and Takhellambam Bokul as the representative to participate in the debate.

As usual the process and nature of the debate was started with an undesirable scene. The debate was initiated first by Pukhrambam Ibomcha. In his presentation he had categorically pointed out the fact that the Meetei Marup as a religious organization never criticized any religion or for that matter any other religious organisation. Their only aim and objective was to make an attempt to promote and foster their primary religion which was closely associated with the birth and death of their forefathers in their own language at the time of the worshipping of god and goddesses. While the deliberation was going on Sibadatta Sharma a member of the panel of debators gave an interruption by asking Ibomcha to show the real identity of the god of their religion. In a very cool and calm voice Ibomcha tried to convince by giving a list of names which were considered by the members of their organization as the god of the primary religion. But due to the frequent interruption by the members of the reprentatives of the Brahmins the whole decorum of the debate was put in a very bad shape. Then exchange of word between the Meetei Marup and Brahmins also had started. At some stages in the process of debate the Brahmin representatives had crossed the official decorum and norms of the debate. It is said that at a particular stage of the debate Sibadatta Sharma said that if the language of the debate was in 'Sanskrit' nobody would be able to stand before him even for five minutes. In the same nature Takhellambam Bokul also said that if the debate was in his mother tongue nobody would be able to stand before him even for three minutes. Thus due to the exchange of heated words between the two groups the nature of the religious debate went down to the degree of the lowest category. To see this ugly situation the president of the debate Shri Sougaijam Somorendro Singh had postponed till the next day.

The second session was held on the next day i.e. 29th June 1950 at the same place. Shri Sinam Krishnamohon Singh had presided over the session. This day also the nature of the debate was not continued with a healthy atmosphere. Repeated interruption and exchange of word among the participants became the nature of the debate. While the debate was going on one Bamon Gouramani Sharma from Kwakeithel area, who was popularly known as 'Kudam Bamon' stood up from the audience side and started to criticize Naoria Phullo.To see his undesirable attitude other people asked the president of the session to stop him as he was not given the permission to speak as an participant. In the meantime one Tomansana from Thangjam Leikai also started to speak against Hindu religion from the audience side. Thus an ugly situation was developed in the course of the debate. To see such type of undemocratic behavior among the debators and audience, the president of the session had compelled Gourmani Sharma to leave the hall immediately. With this the second session also came to an end with great confusion and ugly scene. However the members of Meetei Marup felt that it was their victory because the members of Brahma Sabha were not able to give befitting reply in this religious debate.

Thus in their attempt to revitalize the primary religion of this country the members of Meetei Marup faced a lot obstacles from the Brahma Sabha. Such type of strong resistance from this religious body and resultant conflict had produced serious problems in the harmonious relationship in every aspects of the social life of the people. It was mainly because of the threat from the social ostracism policy of the Brahma Sabha the members of the Meetei Marup and those persons who embraced the practice of primary religion were not allowed to mix up in any social gatherings. They were not allowed to work together with the other people in the cultivation and harvesting seasons. The Meetei Hindu people refused to marry their sons and daughters to the families of those persons who embraced primary religion. Even in the same family also a serious crisis developed between the members pro-and anti-Hindu religion. It is also said that in most of the cases the anti-Hindu members of the family were not allowed to eat live together with the pro-Hindu members under the same roof. They were forced to live in a separate place. Sometimes it also happened that fencing was erected between the land of pro and anti Hindu families. The persons of anti-Hindu elements were debarred from joining the '*Singlup*'[37] of the respective locality. Even they were not allowed to enter and participate at the *Lai Haraoba* festivals which are closely associated with the religious concept and practices of the primary religion. It is also recorded that many people of anti Hindu elements had filed case at the court against those persons who did not allow them to enter and participate the *Lai Haraoba* festival.[38] As a result of this religious conflict, a sharp division was created among the people in every locality. In some areas a parallel '*Singlup*' was started to operate for different religious sect. Thus the

'Mangba and Sengba'(clean and unclean) policy of the Brahma Sabha had produced a serious intolerable problem in the social life of the people of Manipur. Even in the year 1938 this idea of clean and unclean was challenged by Hijam Irabot Singh, a great revolutionary leader of Manipur. It is recorded that in a debate which was held on the 1st August 1938, members of the Brahma Sabha were not able to give a convincing answer to the arguments of Irabot.[39] Thus in the process of religious revitalization movements the members of the Meetei Marup had faced a series of steep resistance from the Brahma Sabha. Apart from this they had also come across a number of minor incidents of conflict which had sometimes created a situation for the growth of sentiments between the people of pro and anti-Hinduism. Whatever may be , it can also be suggested that the strong resistance activities of Brahma Sabha was a sort of undisguised boon in favour of the Meetei Marup. That their action gave a new strength in their effort to revitalize the primary religion and made a good room for the consolidation of their movement.

NOTES

1. Meetei Marup Hourakpa 1945, Khwi Meetei Thoukal Langol Malup, p.1.
2. Sairem Nilbir, *Lainingthou Sanamahi amasung Sanamahi Laining Hingat Ihou,* 2002, p.136.
3. *Ibid.,* p.152.
4. *Ibid.,* p.136.
5. It is a kind of tax introduced and collected by the Brahma Sabha from the Meetei Hindu people.
6. It is a kind of tax collected from the people for cutting the hair at the time of earring and thread bearng ceremony.
7. *Meetei Marup Hourakpa,* 1945, p.1.
8. Sairem Nilbir, *op.cit.,* p.136.
9. Meetei Marup Hourakpa, *op. cit.,* p. 2.
10. *Ibid.*
11. Meetei Marup Hourakpagi Ahanba Tangkak(1945 – 47), Meetei Marup Meetei Leibak, 1993, p. 3.
12. *Ibid.,* p. 4.

13. Meetei Marup Hourakpa, p.4.
14 *Ibid.*
15. Meetei Marup Hourakpagi Wari, *op. cit.*, p.13.
16. *Ibid.*
17. Meetei Marup Hourakpa, *op. cit.*, p.6.
18. Meetei Marup Hourakpagi Wari, *op. cit.*, p. 21.
19. Meetei Marup Hourakpa. *op. cit.*, p.6.
20 *Ibid.*, p.7.
21 Meetei Marup Hourakpagi Wari, *op. cit.*, p.7.
22. *Ibid.*
23 *Ibid.*, p.8.
24. *Ibid.*, p.9.
25. *Ibid.*, p.10.
26. *Ibid.*
27. *Ibid.*, p.11.
28. *Ibid.*, p. 17.
29 *Ibid.*, p.18.
30. *Ibid.*, pp.18-19.
31. *Ibid.*
32. *Ibid.*, p.22.
33. *Ibid.*
34. *Ibid.*, p.23.
35. *Ibid.*, p.24.
36. *Ibid.*, p.28.
37. '*Singlup*' is a voluntary social and religious organization which established for every *Leikai*(locality) by the people of that particular area. Its main objective was to extend all the requisite help to the needy family.
38. Meetei Marup Hourakpagi Wari , *op. cit.*, p.30.
39. *Cheitharol Kumbaba,* p. 629.

6

Nature and Character of the Movement

After having an unprecedented unique experience of unending conflict with the members of the *Brahma Sabha* on the issue of their different religious outlook the leaders of the *Meetei Marup* had diverted their attention towards a more logical and practical approach. Accordingly they had started to concentrate their time and energy for the materialization of their objective. They strongly believed that their aim would be able to achieve only when the religious outlook of the people was changed effectively. Under this concept they had started to pay a serious attention for an alternative to counter the process of Hindu colonialism. In the mean time the whole social and political atmosphere of Manipur also began to change very fast in a more unexpected way. The introduction of new political outlook in the state which was based on the principle of democracy had brought a drastic change in the outlook and mindset of the people. On the other hand, such type of new outlook also began to question the relevance of feudal administrative character in the state. The decline of the importance of feudal elements in the administrative setup also had produced an impact in the character and attitude of the members of the *Maha Sabha*. The transformation in the religious and political outlook of the general public had forced the members of the *Maha*

Sabha to tone down their chauvinistic character in the religious affairs of the state. Such type of new developmental conditions in the religious atmosphere in the state was a great advantageous position to those who had a strong tendency to recall the golden age of the past.

The outcome of the debate between Meetei Marup and Brahma Sabha was indeed, a significant contribution to the religious movement in Manipur. The intensity of the degree of debate was so serious that it produced a large scale impact in the whole social, political and religious environment of the state. On the other hand the emergence of a new political atmosphere also produced a great impact in the thinking process of the people particularly the new generation people. After getting freedom from the clutches of colonial and feudal administration the people who had a strong desire to promote the culture and history of this place, began to give maximum emphasis for the establishment of a distinctive cultural identity of their own, based on the importance of the traditional principles. These people had strongly asserted that the concept and nature of the Hindu religion was the only instrument for the loss of their traditional cultural and religious identity. Therefore, they were of the view that the distinctive identity could be maintained only when their traditional cultural and religious system was preserved under a systematic approach. With this ultimate objective, they began to assert for the promotion and maintenance of various cultural and religious life of this place. To justify their stand they made an intensive and tireless effort to discover many ancient literary texts called *Puyas* which were in the private possession of many individuals. With the help of these written works they were able to give a strong logical justification about their attempt to revitalize the indigenous religion and custom of Manipur.

Though there were many instances of debate between the pro and anti Hindu elements in the society the nature and character of the movement as a whole was based in a more peaceful and democratic way. The people who strongly asserted for the promotion of traditional culture and religion did not force and compel anybody to accept their view point immediately. Rather they had concentrated their campaign only for having an understanding through debate and discussion about the positive and negative aspects of the existing cultural and religious behavior. They also pointed out the historical evidences about the policy adopted by the Hindu preachers for the strengthening of sanskritisation process in Manipur. Thus in a more democratic and non violent way the elements of the anti Hinduism among the people had made a serious attempt to bring changes in the religious and cultural life of the people. However, in spite of their best attempt they were not able to change the mind of the common people very easily. Even they refused to accept the rational and logical arguments placed by the members of the radical section of the society. From this discouraging atmosphere the members of the anti-Hindu organizations felt the immediate need to counter the existing religious concept and practice of Hinduism. In the meantime a number of small organizations had also sprang up in the valley areas with a basic objective to assert for the promotion of the distinctive identity of primary religion against the Hinduism. As a part of their activities they make an attempt to give awareness to the common people about the importance of primary religion with help of the evidences and information mentioned in the written texts. The attempt to publish all the available literaly texts which were scattered in the private custody of individuals was also one of their main activity. Their only objective was to make a new platform through which the common people would be able to make their own judgment about the merits and demerits of the two religious concept and practices. In spite of their best possible efforts they were not able to bring a dramatic change in the mindset of the common people.

To see the discouraging response of the people they were now fully convinced that to make an attempt for a new religious outlook of the common people through dialogue only would not bring any type of positive answer in favour of their efforts. Perhaps they might have an impression that some kind of practical effort should be made so that they would be able to draw the attention of the common people in favour of their attempt. So in order to attract the attention of the people they have decided to foster and promote the religious festivals which was overshadowed by the Hindu religion. As already mentioned above about the policy of the Hindu colonialism under which they made a drastic change on the features and character of the traditional religious festivals to suit Hindu religious way of life. To change the national identity of all the important rivers, hills, lakes and places in the Hindu name and to give the character of Hindu religion in the traditional religious festivals was the basic policy throughte which the preacher of Hinduism was able to consolidate their position in the contry. It is a well known fact that the sanskritisation process was successfully implemented in Manipur with strong patronage of the king. Its influence was so deep rooted that after the adoption of Hindu religion every Manipuri began to look their way of life from the new religious point of view. This was the prevailing situation in the country before the growth of new awareness about the importance of primary religion. They also believed that this notion could be removed only when the degree of the importance and value of the primary religion and custom was fully established in the mindset of the people. With this idea in their mind and as a beginning of the activities the members of the radical section of the society had started to focus on the value and importance of the cultural heroes and heroines of this place. Apart from this they had also paid an attention to reactivate the traditional script against the Bengali script which is now officially used by the people of Manipur. To worship Panthoibi, Imoinu and the observance of New Year etc. are some of the program taken up by these religious organizations as a part of the activities of the religious revitalization movements in Manipur.

1. Worship of Panthoibi in Place of Durga

To worship Goddess Panthoibi in place of Durga a female deity of Hindu religion may be observed as an important step in the process of the religious revitalization movement. Durga Puja as a big religious festival of the Hindu people was introduced in Manipur most probably in the middle of nineteenth century. But the concept of 'Devi' was first introduced by Shanti Das Gossai the moment he failed to destroy the shrine of Hiyangthang Lairembi. It was happened during the time of king Garibniwaz. As a part of the policy of the demolition of the idols of primary religion Shati Das Gossain tried to destroy the place of Hiyangthan Lairembi. But his attempt was completely shattered by the super natural power of the deity. To see the unique power of the deity he immediately stopped the work and declared this religious place as an important religious sacred place of 'Devi' of Sakta Cult. Then he established a new identity of Hiyangthang Lairembi as the '*Goddess Kamakhya*'[1] of Hindu religion. Then at the suggestion of Shanti Das the king of Manipur had entrusted the responsibilities of the proper care of this deity to a Brahmin. From this period the converted Meitei Hindu people worshiped this place as the shrine of the Hindu goddess 'Devi' or 'Durga'. However the worship of the symbolic image of 'Durga'for five days from the day of '*Mera Chaorel Houba*' was perhaps started from the time of king Chandrakriti (1850–1886).[2] But nothing specific about the performance of Durga Puja festival is mentioned in the royal chronicle except the performance of boat festival called 'Nouka Khela' (festival of boat)[3] which was performed at the evening of the last day of Durga Puja. From this evidence it can be suggested that this religious festival perhaps was started from the time of king Chandrakriti. The worship of the symbolic image of Goddess Durga was first performed at the royal palace. Then it gradually spread to other places of the state as an important religious festival. And thus the popularity of the worship of the idol of Durga was increased tremendously and the people also had started to worship Durga in their respective houses. During this period of five days the people had enjoyed all sorts of entertainments like the performance of music, dance etc. Thus from the last quarter of the nineteenth century the Durga Puja festival was performed in a large scale way with a maximum degree of festive mood.

Then from the year nineteenth sixties the anti Hinduism elements among the people began to worship *Panthoibi*, an important female deity in the mythology of the primal religion just to counter of Durga Puja. Such type activities were a new developmental phenomenon in the process of the religious revitalization movement. But still it is quite obscure to understand how a similarity could be established between these two female deities in their respective character and nature. According to the religious concept of the Hindu religion Goddess Durga represents as a symbol of power, protector of justice and destructor of evils. Whereas the *Goddess Panthoibi*, analysing from her various characteristic, may be suggested that she represented the perfect role model of highly mature degree of womanhood. Due to her distinctive various roles she was mystified as a super element having no parentage of her own. In the mythology of the primal religion she was regarded as another form of *Nongthang Leima* who was created for a specific purpose by the Supreme God at the time of the creation of the universe.[4] It may also be mentioned that she was closely associated with every aspects of the life cycle of human beings. The identity of *Goddess Panthoibi* was varied according to the nature of her works. Therefore the similarities with Goddess Durga perhaps, might have been established only when her nature of work was related with the use of weapons and other forms of martial arts. From this angle she was treated as the goddess of war and protector from the evil elements.[5] The worship of *Goddess Panthoibi* was started from the time of King Charairongba (1697-1709).[6] But it is quite obscure to know under which identity she was worshipped as goddess. Some writers were of the view that the establishment of identity of *Nongpok Ningthou and Panthoibi* as the *Mahadeva and Durga* by the Hindu preachers was perhaps due to the similar character and nature between Panthoibi and Durga. So, on the basis of this evidence the members of the anti -Hinduism organisations might have taken the same analogy[7] for their own purpose. However still it is quite obscure to ascertain the actual year of the beginning of the worship Goddess Panthoibi in place of Goddess Durga. But it is said that the worship of Panthoibi was initiated by some anti Hinduism persons of Thangmeiband area in the beginning of nineteen sixties. Since then this religious festival was performed and spread in other areas also. In course of time the popularity of the worship of Panthoibi had increased tremendously. Such type of new phenomenon is indeed a great achievement of the members of the anti Hinduism organisations. Therefore the introduction of the worship of *Goddess*

Panthoibi in place of the *Durga Puja* is a great positive step towards the process of the religious revitalization movement in Manipur.

2. Worship of Goddess Imoinu

To worship *Goddess Imoinu* was also another religious festival which has become a very important program of the religious rervitalisation movement. Actually it is not a new phenomenon but to worship her in a large scale way was a new emerging character in the religious history of Manipur. The importance of Goddess *Imoinu* in relationship to day-to-day life of the people of Manipur has its own historical root. She was intimately related with the material development and economic life of the people. Like *Goddess Panthoibi* she was also treated as another form of identity of *Nongthang Leima.* Accordingly she was regarded as a very peculiar character having no parentage identity of her own. Apart from this she was also known by various forms of identities like the Goddess of 1. Wealth, 2.Granary or paddy, 3. Fish, 4. Water, 5. Salt, 6. Work culture and 7. War.[8] From these several characteristic features she was also treated as a household goddess. Apart from this she was also regarded as a goddess of *'Achi Tattabi'* and *'Arai Kangdabi'.*[9] *i.e.* no dearth of the flow of wealth.

Many references were made in ancient literary texts about the worship of *Imoinu* as the goddess of wealth. During the reign of king Khagemba(1597-1652) and his successor king Khunjaoba the worship of *Imoinu* was made compulsory for every household. It was a very popular religious festival of the country[10] and it was performed annually on the 12th day of the month of Wakching (December and January). On this very day every member of the family worshipped *'Imoinu'* at *'Phunga Lairu'*[11] (fire place) located inside the kitchen room of the house. The offering of fresh vegetables and fruits at the *Phunga Lairu* along with meal specially prepared with a type of fish called *'Sareng'* (wattagu attu), a kind of big and fairly good eating fish is the unique features of the rituals of the worship of Imoinu. It is the common belief among the people that the worship of Imoinu would bring prosperity to the family.

But the importance and popularity of the worship of Imoinu was severely declined just after the introduction of Hindu religion. At the strong pressure of the Hindu preachers, the common people began to give more emphasis to the worship of Lakshmi the Goddess of wealth of Hindu religion. The introduction of *'Dipa Nwita'*, the fire festival had occupied a prominent position in the mindset of the people. The people believed that on this day of fire festival *Goddess Lakshmi* had visited every house. Thus with the establishment of Hindu religion worship of *Goddess Lakshmi* had replaced the position of Goddess *Imoinu.* The ignorance of the importance of the goddess Imoinu in the mindset of the people gradually came to an end with the emergence of the idea of religious revitalization movement among the radical section of the society.

Such type of positive tendency which was developed among the people was further strengthened and intensified by the activities of the elements of anti Hinduism. At the beginning the worship of *Imoinu* was confined only to the limited circles. This trend was continued for about two decades. Then just from the beginning of nineteenth seventies the nature of the worship of *Imoinu* as a goddess of wealth was started in a large scale way. Each and every member of the family had started to perform the religious rites of this goddess with utmost care and respect. In the meantime at the initiative of some interested persons the characteristic feature of the worship of Goddess Imoinu was brought from the 'Phunga Lairu' to the public place and made it a big religious festival. Thus the worship of Imoinu began to cross the boundary of the traditional ritualistic pattern. This is an interesting departure from the old practices. The room for proper attention and attraction of the people to this religious festival was made available by an organization called 'League of Callow Patriots' of Wangkhei Ningthem Pukhri Mapan, Imphal in the year 1978.[12] The members of this organization started to perform the religious festival in a large scale way. It is said that one of the basic objectives of the organization was to foster and promote the rich cultural tradition which were considered to be in a stage of extinction. Under this notion they always put a high degree of importance to the rites and rituals of Goddess Imoinu. Therefore with this sole objective they started to take responsibilities to promote the religious festival of Imoinu from the 12th of Wakching (January/February) of the year 1978. The religious festival was performed with full of enthusiasm and the worshipping area was decorated with torch of fire. The ritual was performed at the place of the deity 'Khulleima' at the Ningthem Pukhri Mapan. Thus gradually the intensity of the degree of the importance of goddess *Imoinu* increased tremendously in every area. Again in the year 1986 another religious organization called '*Inat Khongul Liba Lup*' of Khudrakpam Assembly Constituency had organized a big torch rally in connection with the worship of *Goddess Imoinu*. About seven to eight thousands people had participated in that rally. It was started from the Wakhong village and completed at Waiton village by covering around ten miles. The members of the organization arranged a public meeting with the local M.L.A.[13] The main objective of the rally was to give a strong message to the general people for the promotion of traditional religion and culture for the maintenance of the distinctive identity of the people of this state. In the meantime some enthusiastic people of the Yumnam Leikai area also had started to perform the worship of Goddess Imoinu at the public place. The arrangement was made in such a marvelous way that people were able to enjoy the religious festival with full of satisfaction. Thus the importance of the worship of this goddess had increased tremendously in the mindset of the people. To see the significance of this religious festival in the cultural and religious life of the people of this state and to understand the degree of the involvement of the masses the state government have included the day of the worship of *Goddess Imoinu* as the restricted holiday since 1993. Then in the year 2000 A.D. it was again declared as the general holiday. Such type of development may be treated as a positive aspect of the activities of the religious revitalization movement. Apart from its ritualistic side the orgasnisers also introduced some kind of entertainment items like dance and music etc. Thus the worship of *Goddess Imoinu* became a great religious festival in the state. The involvement of masses across the boundary line of their religious belief itself may be suggested as a great achievement of the members who strongly advocated for the religious revitalisation movement in Manipur.

3. To stop the observation of Saraswati Puja

To worship *Saraswati*, the goddess of learning of the Hindu religion was one of the greatest religious festival, particularly among the student community in Manipur. Apart from the educational institutions the worship of Goddess Swarasati was also performed in several other offices. The introduction of the worship of *Goddess Saraswati* in the educational institution was a direct outcome of the flourishment of the influence of Hinduism in Manipur. It is mentioned that the Saraswati Puja, as a religious festival particularly among the student community was first introduced at Johnstone School[14] which was established in the name of Sir James Johnstone the then British Political Agent in Manipur during 1885-86 A.D. Here it can be recalled how the Bengali teachers involved in the introduction of formal education system in Manipur. Therefore since the schools had started with the Bangali teachers the medium of teaching was also made in Bengali language. It is mentioned that this trend was continued till the 1924.[15] Therefore it may be suggested that the Bengali teachers, perhaps taking the advantage of the fluid situation of that period of time they might have introduced the Saraswati Puja festival in the school. Ultimately it became a very popular religious festival of the student community of the state. The nature of the worship of Swarasati was organised with full of festive mood and the entertainment activities. The religious festival was continued for about two or three days with a full of entertainment programs. During the puja period there were no academic works in the educational institutions.

The nature of the financial involvement in the performance of Saraswati Puja was based mainly from the subscription of money from the student which wsas paid at the time of fresh admission. It was known as 'Puja Fee. But from the beginning of the year 1970 the degree of the celebration of this puja began to decrease very fast. Perhaps it was mainly because of the increased of anti - Hindu activists.

At that time for the performance of Saraswati Puja every educational institution had taken nominal fees from the students. That was known as *Puja Fee*. The guardians who were the strong believer of primal religion had started to question about the nature of the collection of *puja fee* from their children.[16] The event of the refusal to subscribe puja fee by the guardians took place at the school of Ananda Singh Academy, Imphal.[17] From here the ideas against the performance of Swarasati Puja began to spread in other educational institutions. It is also recorded that in the year 1976 students of Dhanamanjuri College of Arts (D.M.College of Arts) had worshipped the '*Goddess Shilleima*' another form of Panthoibi, in place of Goddess Saraswati.[18] Thus with this new emerging idea of anti-Hinduism, the students began to pay less attention to the observance of Saraswati Puja. Gradually the students began to stop the performance of Saraswati Puja in their respective educational institutions. It has already been mentioned above about the importance of this religious festival in the social and religious life of the people. So initially even the State Government included the days of the period of religious festival in the holiday list of the government. But to see the extreme degree of the indignant attitude of the student communities, the state government later on removed the Saraswati Puja from the list of the general holiday and included only in the list of the restricted holiday. Thus in course of time the importance of this religious festival had completely vanished from every educational institutions of the state. However, the members of the anti - Hinduism were not prepared to give another alternative to the observance of Saraswati puja. There are a number of references about the existence of either god or goddesses related with learning and teaching. In this respect some writers were of the opinion that since the religious festival was not directly related with the social and cultural life of the people, perhaps they were not able to give a specific alternative to the Hindu puja. Whatever the case may be, the stopping of the performance of Saraswati Puja completely from the educational institutions was a major breakthrough in the ongoing process of the religious revitalization movement in Manipur.

4. Celebration of New Year on the first day of the month of Sajibu (*Sajibu Nongma Panba Cheiraoba*)

To celebrate the 'New Year' on the first day of the month of Sachiphu or Sajubu (March/April) is also another noteworthy achievement of those people who strongly advocated for the revitalisation of the primary religion. The celebration of New Year is one of the biggest religious and cultural festivals of every country. In Manipur the first day of the New Year is called 'Cheiraoba', 'Chei' means stick and 'Laoba' means to announce. In the early period of time the announcement of the beginning of New Year was performed by a person selected for the purpose by holding a stick in his hand. At the same time it is also recorded that at a particular period of time the announcement of new year was done by four persons selected for the purpose from every 'pana' by holding a stick having a bell on the top of it.[19] But still it is quite obscure to know the exact year of the introduction of the religious and cultural concept of '*Cheiraoba*' in this state. However the announcement of the beginning of the New Year by the four people one each from every 'Pana' was in practiced even before the reign of King Kiyamba (1467-1508). This practice was stopped during the time of king Kiyamba. In his time a new system called '*Cheithaba*' was introduced. The term 'Chei' means 'the stick' and 'Thaba' means 'to count'. That means to count the number of sticks. According to this new system the person who was selected for this specific job have to make an assurance that he would take full responsibilities of all good or bad omen of the country which might have happened during the coming year. This assurance was made in front of the king of the country. One Hiyangloi was the first man to start the work of *Cheithaba*.[20]

Indeed, the celebration of *Cheiraoba* is a very important religious and cultural festival enjoyed by every member of the society with utmost care. Cleaning the house with certain degree of innovation according to the capabilities of the families marked the beginning of the celebration of the *Cheiraoba* (New Year). It is also imperative of every member of the family to maintain an atmosphere of calm and quiet on this very day so that there would be no sign of undesirable tendencies and unhappiness in the family. Just after cleaning the house and other related things fresh vegetable and fruits including some quantity of rice is offered to *Sanamahi*, the household deity. Then a meal is prepared out the food items and is offered to the god before taking meal by the members of the family. A small quantity of prepared food is also offered to the other deities which are known as '*Lamlai*'(Lam means area outside the homestead and Lai means deity) at the gate. Then after taking the meal the people went to the nearby hills to worship deity. Apart from this the married sisters and daughters offered gifts of New Year in kind to their father and brothers. On the other hand for the prosperity of the state the members of the *Maiba Loisang* (Department of priest) also performed the religious rituals of various deities like 1.*Nongsaba*, 2.*Pakhangba* and 3.*Yumjao Lairembi*. The rituals were started right from the early morning and the priests had changed a new cloth of these deities.[21] Then it was followed by the worship of another deity called '*Langol Thongak Lairembi*' at the Langol hill. After this the ancestor deities of three clans *i.e.*, *Mangang*, *Luwang* and *Khuman* was worshipped by the priests by offering new vegetables and fruits.[22] It is also a common belief among the people that the performance of these rites and rituals would bring peace and prosperity to the state. Another very peculiar feature of the observance of New Year Day is the introduction of the concept of 'Silhenba' system. *Sil* means work and *henba* means to stop i.e. to stop the work of the day. It is said that at the early period of time 'Silhenba' was performed for five days. During this period of days the people enjoyed the time by playing '*Kang*'a kind of indigenous game.[23] The new year celebration is followed by another ritual called '*Kongba Leithong Phatpa Sajibu Leikhun Phunba*'. This is also another important part of the celebration of New Year. This ritual is performed on the seventh day of the month of '*Sajibu*'(March/ April) to examine the good and bad sides which might have been fallen upon the people during the current year. Thus right from the very beginning the people had observed the *New Year* day rituals with full of proper care and entertainments.

The emergence of Hinduism as a state religion had brought a dramatic total change in the basic nature and character of the celebration of *New Year*. The day of the celebration of New Year was also changed from the first day of the month of Sajibu to the '*Charak Puja*' of the Hindu religion. It is mentioned that this religious function is performed mostly in Bengal and other adjoining areas. It is called the '*Maha Vishnu Sankranti*'.[24] The performance of the rites and rituals of the new year on the day of the '*Charak Puja*' was perhaps started from the beginning of the eighteenth century i.e., just after the flourishment of Hinduism in Manipur. It is also said that the celebration of *New Year* on the day of 'Charak Puja' of Bengal was introduced from the 18th century.[25] Such type of sharp changes from traditional character to the system of Hindu religion was closely observed by many writers with critical assessment. They were of the view that such type of changes had produced a great confusion in the distinctive character of the primal religion. As has already been mentioned above, the worship of the deities by the people was done after taking their lunch. The people used to go to the nearby hills to worship the deities as a part of the celebration of New Year. But under the influence of Hinduism all the deities were identified as the 'Mahadeva' a deity of Hindu religion. The concept lingered in the mindset of the common people for quite long time. Such type of situation was regarded by the people of anti-Hindu organizations as a serious encroachment to the basic identity of the primal religion. Therefore to protect and foster the real nature of the religion and custom of the people, the leaders of the revitalisastion movement have strongly asserted to bring a complete change in the nature of the system of Cheiraoba.

With these sole objective they had started to perform New Year on the first day of the month of Sajibu (March and April) which was a practice in the country b fore the coming of Hinduism. It was popularly known as *Sajibu Nongma Panba*. But from the beginning of nineteenth sixties the number of families who performed 'Cheiraoba' on the first day of the month of Sajibu was tremendously increased. In the mean time some organizations who strongly advocated for revitalising the primary religion of Manipur took an initiative to bring a complete change in the character of 'Cheiraoba' from Hinduism to primary religion. The names of the organizations were 1. Hourakpham Thijinba Kanglup, 2. Sajibu Nongma Panba Cheirao Thoupang Lup, 3. Inat Kanba Lup, 4. Leimaron Sintha Marup, 5. Chatnarol Thigatpa Kanglup, 6. Noth Eastern Cultural Research Association, 7.Kanglei Inat Kanba Phurup and 8. Sajibu Nongma Panba Cheiraoba Ad hoc Committee. They formed a Joint Action Committee with an objective to work together for the fulfillment of their common objective. The name of the committee was known as the *Sajibu Nongma Panba Cheiraoba Ad hoc Committee.* From this platform they made a circulation to all the people of Manipur to observe the 'Cheiraoba' festival on Monday the 17th March 1980[26] *i.e.* the first day of the month of Sajibu. Along with this they also requested the State Government to declare the first day of the month of Sajibu or Sajibu Nongma Panba as the general holiday. The state Government also, perhaps sensing the gravity of the importance of this day from the religious and cultural point of view and also sensing the strong intention of the masses, had given a good response to their request. Accordingly the government had declared the 'Sajibu Nongma Panba' as the restricted holiday. Thus gradually the performance of 'Cheiraoba' on the first day of Sajibu had increased in an unexpected way. Even the families of Meetei Hindu people also began to join this religious festival. From the year 1980 the activities of the '*Sajibu Nongma Panba Cheiraoba*' began to spread like a wild fire. In the year 2000 A.D. the State government had declared this day as *'Meetei Cheiraoba'*. Even the important persons in the administration like Governor of the State and Chief Minister also started to recognize this festival by giving message to the people in connection with this religious festival. Thus to bring a complete transformation in the character of 'Cheiraoba' from the practices of Hinduism to primary religion is a great notable achievement of the leaders and other members of the various organizations who strongly advocated for the revitalization of the primary religion.

5. Reintroduction of Manipuri script

The movement for the reintroduction of Manipuri script was also another important landmark of the religious revitalization movement in Manipur. It is recorded that for the first time the script was introduced during the time of King Khagemba. Since then the people used to write in this script. But the importance of the traditional script was gradually eroded with the increase of the influence of Hinduism. And this changing phenomenon was further strengthened by the introduction of British colonial administration. In this respect it can be suggested that rapid decline of the importance of traditional script was more or less directly related with the long absence of the formal education system in the country. From the pages of the history it can be evidenced that even though the script was introduced there were no system of formal education in the country from the real sense of the modern terminology. There might have been many reasons behind this. But the general people were not able to acquire the real test about the importance of the script. Rather its benefit was confined only to the small group of people who were actively involved in the writing and maintaining the ancient texts called 'Puya'. This situation perhaps may be a strong factor for the penetration of the influence of foreign script in the country. The fact was clearly demonstrated by the historical process of later years. The increase of strong influence of Hinduism had brought a revolutionary change in the whole life of the people and its impact was felt in all aspects of their outlook. Ultimately the people began to give more importance either to the Sanskrit or Bengali language and script which were closely related with the new religion. So when the colonial administrators introduced formal education system they faced a great problem of the lack of the persons who could take up the teaching job. To meet the immediate need of the situation the colonial administrators were compelled to take help of the people coming from outside the country. In this situation the teachers coming from Bengal played a predominant part in the expansion of the modern and formal education system in the country. Indeed the introduction of mass education system in the nineteenth century had produced two important impacts. One aspect was related with the flourishment of Bengali script as the official script of the state and other aspect was the sharp decline of the distinctive character of the traditional script. So the modernization of education system of the country with the help of the teachers from outside the country and importance given to the Bengali script may be observed as the key factor for the sharp decline of the existence of traditional script among the people.

However with the coming of the idea of revitalization of the concept and practice of the primal religion against what may be called as religious colonialism, the idea of the importance of traditional script was also developed in the minds of the people. The initiatives were taken by some people who strongly advocated for the maintenance of the identity of the people. They strongly asserted that there was every possibility for a sharp change in the outlook of the society particularly in the fields of the cultural and religious identities if the position of the traditional script was in a proper shape. They were also of the view that to reactivate or reintroduce the traditional script would be stepping stone towards the process of the revitalisation of the primal religion and its associated cultural elements. Within the framework of this belief they had started to take initiative for the reintroduction of the traditional script in place of Bengali. The first state level conference on the traditional script was held in the year 1958. It was known as '*Mayek Luptin Conference*'.[27] It was organized under the initiative of one Thokchom Thoukanchanba. The participants in the conference, after having a detail discussion, agreed to adopt the twenty-seven alphabets to replace the existing Bengali alphabets. But other groups were not in favour of the resolution of the conference. Thus the debate was continued for quite long time. Whatever the case may be, this conference may be treated as a very important step towards the process of the reintroduction and popularization of traditional script against the existing one which is officially used by the people. Thus from this time onwards the anti-Hindu organizations had made a continuous effort to change the script from Bengali to traditional script. Again in the year 1969 a big conference on the identification and fixation of the number of alphabets of the traditional script was held at Mapal Kangjeibung, Imphal from 12th to 23rd February.[28] It was indeed a significant and dramatic development in the process of the identification of the number of alphabets. In the introductory remark the motive of the conference was clearly spelt out in a more logical and rational way. It is said that "Human communities having their own scripts feel happy and also feel proud of writing their own language in their own script. The Meeteis also have a distinct script of their own and as such it is a legitimate claim of the Meeteis for writing Manipuri language in their own Manipuri script. It is quite legal that one ought to pursue and acquire one's own right. Rights do not come automatically and that cannot be exercised if not demanded and acquired. As right is to be demanded there is necessity of demanding the right, there is no wrong in demanding one's right."[29]

Indeed this conference was a major breakthrough in the ongoing attempt of the introduction the traditional script of Manipur and identification of the number of alphabets. In regard to the problem of the confusion in the establishment of the number of alphabets of the traditional script it is said that this situation was created mainly due to the crept of foreign pattern of script in the original number. In this respect it is also observed that long absence of the using of their own script in a large scale way and strong wave of the cultural domination coming from outside was the main reason for the creation of this confusion. The general impression among the people especially to those persons who were actively involved in this issue was that in course of time there might have been so many deletion and addition in the original numbers of alphabets. Therefore the basic objective of the conference was to place genuine alphabets of traditional script by removing all the complicated and controversial issues. As a whole this conference had rendered a big priceless contribution in the attempt to identify a concrete and comprehensive picture of traditional script of this state.

In spite of their best possible efforts still a unanimous conclusion could not be reached on the fixation of the number of alphabets. In the meantime, some enthusiastic people also tried to bring a final acceptable number of the alphabets from the platform of their organizations. Their names were: - 1. Kangleipak Thousinkon, 2. Meetei National Front and 3. Kanglei Eyek Kanba Lup etc.[30] On the other hand the student bodies particularly 'All Manipur Students Union (AMSU)' also made a strong demand to replace the Bengali script by traditional alphabets of this place. Thus the issue of the replacement of Bengali script became an important problem of the state government. The prevailing situation of inconclusive character on the issue of identification of the number of alphabets had invited a number of undesirable tensions among the people. When this was the condition, the state government, with the objective of bringing a final shape, had officially recognized the script of twenty-seven alphabets in the year 1980.[31] Just after getting the official recognition they have made an attempt to introduce the traditional script of twenty-seven alphabet in the schools of primary level. Indeed, the demand to reintroduce the indigenous script was a major breakthrough in the ongoing process of the religious revitalization movement in Manipur. In fact the reintroduction of the original script had further strengthened the intensity of the movement for having a distinctive cultural and religious identity of the people of this state.

While the degree of the intensity of the movement for the reintroduction of indigenous script was moving towards a more critical stage some organizations have started a strong campaign to change the present name of this state. The present name 'Manipur' was made popular from the time of King Garibniwaz.[32] Before that this place was known by several names. The names were Namthak Saronpung, Tilli Kokton Ahanba, Mira Pokthoklam, Hanna Semba Konna Loiba Tillikok Laikoiren, Muwapalli, Chakpa Langba, Wangam Tanthong Mayung Kuiba Maphei Pakpa etc.[33] They were of the view that the existence of this present Hindu name was a great stumbling block in the ongoing process towards the establishment of a distinctive religious and cultural identity of the people who were suppressed for quite long time under the religious colonialism of Hinduism. Therefore they had strongly asserted to change the Hindu name 'Manipur' by the indigenous word of this people. Taking the advantage of the new developmental phenomenon the people in their own ways and desire began to call the state by various names like the '*Kangleipak*', the '*Poireipak*', the '*Meitrabak*'etc. They claimed that these names were closely associated with the evolution of the society. Therefore they strongly asserted that these names would be more appropriate to replace the present name 'Manipur'. The intensity of the degree of campaign to change the name of this place had increased from the period of nineteenth seventies. But, since the matter involves the acceptance of the general population, the idea to change the name of this place is not yet materialised officially. On the other hand the people particularly younger generation have narrowed down the numbers from three to one and expressed their desire to name this state as '*Kangleipak*'. At their own initiative even the people began to use this name in the signboards of shops and hotels and other places of entrepreneurships. Thus the movement to change the name of this place also may be treated as an important part in the ongoing process of the religious revitalization movements in Manipur.

In the meantime the momentum of the anti-Hinduism feeling had increased tremendously among the people of the state. Their only desire was to foster and maintain the distinctive cultural and religious identity of this state. They also believed that this could be possible only when they were completely free from the hypnotized influence of the religious practices of Hinduism which was well developed, and this event is called the *Nongkhran Iruppa.* They also thought that their idea and objective could be made possible only when the religious influence of Hinduism which was injected forcibly against the desire of the people was removed from their mindset. Accordingly with a firm objective to free the mind of the people from the prison of the religious ideology and practices of Hinduism they performed a function called '*Nongkhrei Pareihanba*' in the year 1974 A.D. Thus from this time onwards those radical people began to change the character of the revitalization movements towards a more militant way.

6. Nongkhrei Pareihanba

It was a new form of social movement directed against the

religious practices of Hinduism. This particular event was more or less directly related with the event of *Nongkhrang Iruppa.* As it has already been mentioned above about the importance of this event in relation with the establishment of the authority of Hinduism in Manipur. On this very day the people were forced to embrace the idea and principles of Hindu religion. As a part of the process the common people were asked to take bath at the confluence of Imphal River at Lilong by holding a branch of Nongkhrei plant in their hands. But still it is quite obscure to understand the inner meaning or implication of this plant in relation with the bathing and acceptance of new religion. It is also said that the Hindu preachers asked them to chant the name of 'Shri Ram' a mythical hero of the epic Ramayana.[34] However on the contrary nothing specific is recorded in the royal chronicle about the involvement of general people on the day of the event of Nongkhrang Iruppa. It simply mentioned that on the new moon day of the month of Wakching (December / January) the members of the royal family and Hindu preachers took bath at Lilong and thread ceremony also was held on that day.[35] Whatever the case may be, it is a fact that from that particular event the people began to follow the new religion and its way of life.

According to another version on the new moon day of the month of Wakching , at the royal order of the king, all the people of the state and Hindu preachers took bath at Lilong. Then at the midnight of the same day all the people who took bath at Lilong again performed the same system at Nungjeng Pukhri(it is a name of a pond) inside the Kangla. This particular event was also known as 'Nongkhrang Iruppa'.[36] Then just after taking bath all the people made a promise that they would not give up the 'Mayang Dharma' (foreigners religion) throughout their life.[37] While this forceful process for acceptance of Hindu religion was going on, two persons had refused to obey the order of the king on the pretext that if they accepted new religion their food habit would change and ultimately it would bring down their health position in a miserable condition. Their names were Oinam Marei and Sembang Kutlei. For disobeying the order of the king they were severely beaten by one royal officer called Haobam Selungba. Finally they were forced to take bath in Nungjeng Pukhri by holding a branch of Nongkhrei plant.[38] Having no other alternative to the forceful imposition from the ruler the dejected and helpless people had started to accept the religious ideas and practices of foreign religion on the condition that they would follow the religion only for seven generations starting from the time of King Garibniwaz. And the moment it crossed one day of the stipulated time they would go back to their primary religion. It is said that the king also accepted the condition placed by the people. From this deal also this event was also known as *Nongkhrang Washak* (promise with Nongkhrang). Whatever the case may be, to the members of the anti-Hindu organizations this particular event was a very important historical evidence for giving justification of their activities against the religious colonilistic attitude of the Hindu preachers. They strongly asserted that such type of imposition of religious belief against the desire of the people was the reason for the loss of distinctive religious and cultural identity of the indigenous people of this place.

They also believed that the distinctive character of the society could be restored only when they were free from the promises made by the people on the day of *Nongkhrang Iruppa.* Accordingly they organised a function called *Nongkhrang Pareihanba* in February 1974. The literal meaning of this term means to untie the knot of promises made by the people by holding a branch of Nongkhrei plant. Some writers suggested that the term Nongkhrang Pareihanba should be read as 'Sari Pareihanba' which means to untie the promise.[39] The members of the anti Hindu organisations also claimed that the issue of 'seven generations' from the time of King Garibniwaz had already crossed the stipulative time. Therefore they had a rightful claim and sound logical reason in their attempt to revitalize the concept and practices of primal religion. Their only objective was to bring a general awareness among the people about the history of how the people were forced to embrace foreign religion and importance of Nongkhrang Iruppa in the process of the flourishment of Hinduism. On the basic foundation of this historical event they urged the people to go back again to the concept and practices of primal religion so that they would be able to maintain the distinctive religious and cultural identity in their own way. On the basis of these solid arguments they strongly emphasized the immediate need to organizer the 'Nongkhrang Pareihanba'as a basic foundation to get themselves free from the clutches of the religious exploitation of Hinduism.

The 'Nongkhrang Pareihanba' function was organised on Wednesday the 6th February 1974 at Lilong. It was a well attended function and a large number of people from all directions of the state also came to participate in it. To perform the rites and rituals according to the religious norms of primal religion and special appearance of Shri Okendrajit Singh, son of the late King Budhachandra Singh was the significant person of the function. His participation at the function as a member of the royal family and also as a customary head of the state had produced an important impact in favour of the anti Hindu organizations. On that very day, by taking the advantage of his social and customary statutory position he read out a paper in which he made certain amendments in the rules and regulations to be followed by the *'Pundit Loisang'(* writers department) of the royal court.[40] To the members of the anti-Hindu organizations, this particular function was very important because they had the strong conviction that from this very moment they were able to uncoil the knot of promises reluctantly made by the people at the time of *Nongkhrang Iruppa.* They also thought that after this function they were now completely free from the hypnotism of the magic wane of the religious practice of Hinduism. Indeed, the *'Nongkhrang Pareihanba'* function may be taken as some kind of direct confrontation against the existing religious concept and practices of Hinduism. And this particular religious function had drawn a clear-cut ideological battle line between the elements of Hinduism and primal religion.

Then after a long gap of eighteen years i.e., in the year 1992 Maharajkumar Okendrajit Singh again made an announcement for a complete change in the religious and cultural life of the people. This was known as *'Declaration of Revival'* (Parei Hanba). In this circulated paper, although he had no political status in the state, he declared himself as the king of Manipur. Still it is not clear about the pretext of the using of this position. In his declaration he said that from the 23rd April 1992 i.e. the 21st day of the month of Sajibu (March/April) all the traditional religious and customary practices which were suppressed and subdued by the Hindu religious practices were restored.[41] He introduced the idea of '*Parei Hanba*' (revive)in the interest of the people. After giving a detailed picture of the whole historical process about the nature of the emergence of the Hinduism and role of the kings of Manipur against the desire of the people he further said, "I opened the *Lubak Tabu*(basket) and abandoned Hinduism as State religion and recognition hereby withdrawn from the Royal Customary law of the country; instead the Royal Customary Law revived '*Lainingthouism*' as the State religion and do hereby given recognition as the State religion."[42] The *Royal Declaration of Revival* further mentioned about the restoration of all the properties of the primary religion either in kind or customary courts which were under the control of the religious practices of the Hinduism. Besides, it also mentioned about the restoration of some important religious places to their original name. For example the Hindu name Mahaballi to Mongba Hanba, Kamakhya to Hiyangthang Lairembi, Baruni Mahadeva to Nongpok Ningthou Apanba, Thangjing Mahadeva into Thangjing Lainingthou, Javista to Pakhangba etc.[43] Another notable feature of the 'Declaration' was the assertion for having a unitary body of Hills and Plain peoples which were severely divided by the Hindu religious leaders on the basis of the social ostracism policy. It has also pointed out that there should be no question of the concept of untouchable among the hill and plain people which were enforced by the preachers of Hindu religion. Apart from this Maharajkumar Okendrajit as a head of the customary law of the country had given an assurance to the people of the state that he would strictly exercise the custom and religious law of the traditional practices for the future welfare of the people and country.[44]

Indeed the performance of 'Nongkhrei Pareihanba' function was a great stride towards the positive direction for having a successful religious revitalization movement. The action of these anti Hinduism organizations may be taken as a direct challenge to the existing religious practices of Hinduism and also may be treated as the beginning of the confrontation against the people who were the staunch believer in Hinduism. On the other hand, the active participation and involvement of an important personality of the royal family members who was once the protector of Hindu religion and practices had rendered a valuable contribution in the process of the strengthening of the religious revitalization movement in Manipur.

7. Violent conflict over the possession of Sanamahi

After this historic event the character of the movement began to change towards a more violent nature. It is a well known fact that the sole objective of the anti Hinduism organizations was to bring a complete transformation in the identity of all the sacred religious places in the state and nature of the worship which was completely under the control of the Hindu religious practices. Their first attempt was to control the authoritative and possessive right of the worship of Sanamahi an important deity of primary religion which was closely associated with the cosmogony of this place. Therefore right from the growth of the concept of religion the people began to worship it as their protector. It is recorded that the symbolic idol of God Sanamahi was established during the period of king Khagemba (1597-1652 A.D.). But with the tremendous increase of the influence of Ramandi cult under the initiative of one Santidas Gossain the idol of Sanamahi was completely destroyed during the period of king Garibniwas (1709-1748A.D.). This particular event was a great significant in the entire history of Manipur and still the people always remembered it as the 'SaṇamahiKoluYaikhaiba' (destruction of the image of Sanamahi). The anti-Hindu organizations had utilised this event as a focal point in their attempt to revitalise the primary religion of this place. It is also mentioned that the destruction of the image of Sanamahi brought a very bad ailment to the body of the queen and sons. To see the bad effect of ailment king Garibniwaz immediately ordered to reconstruct the image of god Sanamahi in the same pattern. Thus the image was again constructed. But the responsibility of the proper care of the deity was given to the Brahmin. Thus from the time of king Garibniwaz the responsibilities of the proper care of the deity was given to the care of a Brahmin and this tradition was continued till the year 1975-76. When there was a great demand for the possessive right of God Sanamahi by the members of the anti Hinduism organizations the idol of Sanamahi was in the house of Leihaothabam Surjamani Sharma of Keishamthong Moirangningthou Leirak Imphal.

To perform the rites and rituals of God Sanamahi according to the primordial religious practices of this place, not by the Hindu religious practices was the only desire of the anti-Hindu organisations. They thought that the inability of the people to assert for the establishment of their distinctive identity was mainly due to the worship of God Sanamahi by the Brahmin through their religious concept and practices. Therefore they strongly believed that people would be able to free themselves from the conflicting mindset in their identity only when God Sanamahi was kept and worshipped at his original place. Accordingly the volunteers and members of the various anti Hindu organizations made a massive preparation to carry out the idol of God Sanamhi forcibly from the residence of the Brahmin on the day of *Mera chaorel Houba* in the month of October 1975. The possibilities of the outbreak of the conflict between the anti and pro - Hinduism elements were a serious concern to the state government. Therefore to avoid ant possible disturbances in the law and order situation of the state the government had carefully observed the movement of the people. According to their plan a large number of people went to the house of Leihouthabam Surjamani Sharma to take back the idol of God Sanamahi. To control the situation the police had apprehended about one hundred fifty people and the crowd were dispersed immediately. Thus their first attempt to control possessive authority of the worship of God Sanamahi was ended without any positive result in favour of them. Then in the next year the members of the anti Hindu organizations again prepared to control the religious authoritative right of the worship of Sanamahi. The state government also had received the prior information about their plan. So in order to keep everything under the control the government had promulgated section 144 under Cr.P.C. in the surrounding areas where the idol of Sanamahi was kept. However on 24th September 1976 at about 2.30 p.m. a large number of people had violated the restriction and rushed towards the residence of Leihaothabam Surjamani Sharma to take out the idol of Sanamahi from that place. Without having any other alternative and to control the mob the police opened fire and accordingly two youths were killed. Their name was Heisnam Kumar Singh of Heingang village and Oinam Chaoba of Oinam village. The police also arrested seven persons. Chingsubam Akaba the Chairman of Meitei National Front (M.N.F.) was one of them.

The issue became very serious and it was discussed in the State Legislative Assembly. The on the 3rd December 1976 the Minister of Local Self Government introduced a bill in the assembly for having a separate body to perform the religious rites and rituals of God Sanamahi. It was known as '*Lainingthou Sanamahi Temple Bill*'. After passing in the Assembly it became an Act in the year 1977. The main objective of the Act was to change the possessive right of the worship of God Sanamahi from the Brahmin to a Board to be constituted for that purpose. After getting formal acceptance of the right to worship Sanamahi according to the tradition religious rites and rituals the leaders and volunteers of the anti Hindu organizations went to the residence of Surjamani Sharma on 28th September 1977. But Surjamni Sharma did not allow them to enter in his residence. Immediately the intervention from the side of the government came in favour of the anti Hindu organizations. Accordingly the idol of God Sanamahi was brought from the house of Brahmin Surjamini to the old temple located inside the present area of First Manipur Rifle on the 13th October 1977. Before the establishment of colonial administration this area was known as Tollong Leikai.This particular day is regarded by the members of the anti Hinduism organsations as a great historic day in the ongoing process of the religious revitalization movement in the state.

After having a very good experience of a successful achievement in their violent type of movement they had started to take up a series of attempt to control all the religious sacred places in the state which was used by the Brahmins as an important place of Hindu religion. The occupation of the possessive right of the worship of *'Kongmaru'* or *'Kongba Maru'* as an important religious place located at about 16 K.M.to the north of the upstream of Kongba River was also another notable achievement of the members of the anti-Hindu organizations. It is said that in ancient time this area was known as the place of *'Konjil Tingthokpa Konglouton Louthiba'* a mythical hero of this place.[53] However right from the middle of nineteenth century at the influence of Hinduism the people had started to worship this place as an important abode of God Siva Mahadeva of Hindu religion.[45] Then from the year 1979 the members of anti Hindu organizations had launched a movement to control this place as a sacred place of primal religion. They formed a committee called *'Kongba Maru Laipham Thoupu Kanglup'*. A minor clash took place between the two groups. Finally on 22nd March 1979 the worshipper of God Sanamahi was able to control this place. Then it was followed by the attempt to control the religious sacred place of *Mongba Hanba* areas which is located at the eastern bank of the Imphal River. This area became an important religious place of Ramandi Cult from the time of King Garibniwas. At the influence of the Brahmin the king had established a symbolic idol of Hanuman a monkey hero of epic Ramayan. It is also recorded that the idol was constructed by the big stone slab erected at the market place. From this event this area was popularly known as the' Mahaballi Forest' (Mahaballi Umang). As a part of the program of their religious revitalization movement the leaders and members of the anti Hindu organizations had made up their mind to take the worshipping right of this place. Accordingly they formed a committee called *'Mongba Hanba Umanglai Kanba Lup'* on 6th May 1979. Under the banner of this organization they made a series of attempt to control this place. Sensing the possible danger in the law and order problem the government as a part of the precautionary measure had promulgated Section 144 Cr.P.C. in the surrounding area of this place. In the meantime a series of clash took place between the agitators and police. For the violation of the restriction the government had arrested some leaders of the organizations. Thus the attempt to control the worshipping right of this place between the anti and pro Hinduism elements of the society was continued for quite long time. But all the efforts of the members of the anti-Hindu organizations to control the worshipping right of this religious place was not able to achieve in a more satisfactory way. Gradually the degree of the tempo of the activities also died down. However though they were not able to get an expected positive result, their efforts had given a good contribution in the process of awareness among the general people about the importance of this place. Such type of development also may be treated as a good step towards the direction of the achievement in their attempt to recall the importance of the primary religion and custom.

From the clash over the possessive right of Mongba Hanba, the members of the anti Hindu organizations again had turned their attention towards the religious sacred place of the abode of Nongpok Ningthou which is located at the top of the hill of Nonmgmaiching Hill which is also popularly known as Baruni hill. This place was regarded by these people as the most important religious place. The people believed this place as the coronation site of Nongpok Ningthou and Panthoibi who was regarded as the king of the gods[46] like God Indra of Hindu religion. It is also another belief among the people that on this very day Nongpok Ningthou being the king of the heaven had distributed the spiritual elements in order to get the longevity of age to the human beings. Under this firm belief people went to this religious sacred place to get the blessing of the god for the the longevity of their age. But before going direct to the abode of Nongpok Ningthou people took bath in the stream of water which flows from the main entrance point of the cave and runs towards the north eastern side.a river stream flows towards the north eastern side. It is called 'Chingoi River'. People also regarded this river as important religious sacred place.

But the nomenclature of this religious place was changed during the reign of King Chandrakirti Singh (1850-1886). From this period onwardsthe worship of Nongpok Ningthou and bathing ceremony of Chingoi river was known as the 'Chingoi Baruni'.[47] Then God Nongpok Ningthou was identified as the Lord Mahadeva of Hindu.

The responsibilities of the proper care and management of this religious place was given to the Brahmin. Thus from this period of time the celebration of '*Chingoi Baruni*' became a very important religious festival of Hindu religion. However with the growth of the idea of the religious revitalization movements in Manipur, the people who were actively involved in this process had started to control this religious place. Their activities were started from the year 1978. They forcibly stopped the role played by the 'Govindaji Temple Board' in every important religious place. The volunteers of anti-Hindu organizations particularly of *Meetei National Front* (MNF) had made all the security arrangements carefully on the day of the *Chingoi Irruppa* and worship of the Nongpok Ningthou. In the meantime another organization called '*Nongpok Ningthou Thougal Lup*' had emerged with a sole objective to control the abode of Nongpok Ningthou. In the year 1997 their objective was fulfilled by controlling the worshipping place of Nongpok Ningthou. Apart from this, the organization was able to control all the important religious sacred places which were located in the area of Andro village. Thus the members of the anti-Hinduism organizations had brought a new shape to the character of the religious festival of Chinggoi Iruppa.

From these above historical evidences it can be safely observed that the reactivisation of traditional religious festivals and the attempt to reintroduce the traditional script were the main feature of the religious revitalization movements in Manipur. The patriotic tireless and militant efforts of the members of the different anti-Hindu organizations had produced a dramatic change in the entire social, religion and cultural life of the people. It was mainly because of their serious attempt that the general people had got an opportunity to make their own comparative assessment about the merits and demerits of the Hindu religious way of life vis-à-vis the concept and practices of the primary religion. Thus the successful attempt to reactivate the religious festival of primary religion had rendered a valuable contribution in the process towards a complete religious transformation in Manipur.

NOTES

1. N. Khelchandra Singh, *Ariba Manipuri Sahityagi Itihas,* 1992, p. 38.
2. L. Ibungohal Singh (Ed.), *Cheitharol Kumbaba,* p.334 N. Khelchandra Singh.
3. Irom Amubi Singh, *Leihou Naophamlon,* 1981, p.29.
4. N. Kangjia Mangang, *Panthoibi Thilel,* 2000, p.7.
5. L. Ibungohal Singh (Ed.), *Cheitharol Kumbaba,* pp.62-63 N. Khelchandra Singh.
6. *Ibid.*
7. Sairem Nilbir, *Lainingthou Sanamahi Amasung Sanamahi Laining Hingal Ihou,* 2002, p. 195.
8. *Imoinu Amasung Manipur Pub.* By The League of Callow Patriots in 2226 p.6.
9. *Ibid.*
10. *Ibid.*, p7.
11. It is a place located to the immediate western side of the 'Phunga '(fire place) which is regarded as a religious sacred place by the Manipuris.
12. League of Callow Partiots, *op. cit* (Note of editor)
13. Sairem Nilbir, *op. cit.*, p.196.
14. Thockchom Mangoljao, *Manipurda Nongchuplomgi Sikha Pub.* 1898 Quoted in Sairem Nilbir, p.197.
15. Sairem Nilbir, *op. cit.*, p.196.
16. *Ibid.*
17. *Ibid.*
18. *Ibid*., p197.
19. In the early period administration of Imphal area was divided into four units or 'Panas'. They were 1. Yaiskul Pana 2. Khurai Pana 3. Khwai Pana 4.Wangkhei Pana.
20. *Cheitharol Kumbaba*, p.20.
21. Meitei Harao Kummeigi Seminar paper. Universial Literary Association, 1980, p.58.
22. *Ibid.*, p. 59.
23. Th. Madhop Singh, *Khunung Lichai Sajat,* 2006 p.10 N.Khelchandra Singh.
24. Keisham Birchand Singh, *Cheiraoba,* 2000, p. 7.

25. Sairem Nilbir, *op.cit.,* p. 190.
26. Huyen Lanpao (Local newspaper) 17.3.1980.
27. *Khorirol* No. 5 August 1980, p.15.
28. The Recommandation of Mayek Conference.
29. *Ibid.*
30. Khoirirol, *op.cit.*, p.16.
31. Manipur Gazette No. 33 April 22, 1980.
32. O. Bhogeshwor , *Sanamahi Laikon*, p.50.
33. Khulem Chandrasekhar, *Inatki Harao Kummei*, 1994, p.I.
34. Sairen Nilbir, *op.cit.*, p.166.
35. *Cheitharol Kumbaba*, p.90.
36. Angomba, *Sembi Mukaklei*, p.25.
37. *Ibid,* 27.
38. Nongthonbanha Angou Luwang, *Ningthou Keyambalon*, 1976, p.8.
39. Khumancha Puyam Iboton, *Kanglei Lik, Muthatlakpa*, 1975, p.2.
40. Declaration of Revival (Pari Hanba).
41. *Ibid.*
42. *Ibid.*
43. *Ibid.*
44. Sairem Nilbir, *op.cit.*, p.175.
45. *Ibid.*
46. Moiranthem Chandra Singh, *Panthoibi Khongul* (1972) R.
47. Irom Amubi, *Meitei Thouri Lichal* , 1970.

7

Conclusion

Indeed the successful attempt of Naoria Phullo to revitalize the philosophy and concept of primal religion from the platform of 'Apokpa Marup' and consistent effort to translate the whole idea into a composite and concrete form under the banner of 'Meitei Marup' was a great landmark to the growing political and social consciousness in the state. His inner idea to reopen the chapter of history of this state was really a significant contribution in the process of maintaining the distinctive identity of the people by recalling the glory of the past and her distinctive historical tradition. It is a known fact that the activities of Naoria Phullo were a mass involvement action which asked for a new idea and outlook against the existing order. Therefore since his activities had directly related with the involvement of the masses it had reflected the character of the 'movement'. It is also a commonly accepted view that the term 'movement' is a series of actions and endeavours by a body of persons for a specific purpose. In the case of Naoria Phullo his basic aim was bring a complete change in the social order of the state. Therefore in order to get a positive achievement the whole activities of the movement move through certain natural processual stages. These stages were observed by the social scientists as the basic platform for the outbreak of any type of movement. They further classified this stage as the period of stress and anxiety. They were of the view that if these stages were not effectively fulfilled then any type of movement may not be able to reach its goal to the best possible expectation. In a sense it can be suggested that this period is very important because during this stage the people would take the opportunity to analyse the value of the existing social order to give a new concept and idea for getting more satisfying needs. It is also historically true that people launched the movement for getting a new best alternative against the existing system only when they were matured enough both conceptually and physically. The people would get this idea only when they had come across a series of conflicts which was brought about by the existing social, economic and external forces. And this situation had produced a serious negative impact and ultimately it led for the outbreak of individual stress. The individuals were forced by this environment to test the value judgment of the existing methods and practices in the society. On the other hand the desire of the individual to get more satisfactory needs and help had increased tremendously. This stage is observed by the social scientist as a dangerous stage because if the deteriorating conditions are not checked it would lead to the death of the society. They also suggested that such type situation could be safe only the people had launched the 'revitalisation movement' with a strong radical concept.

In the history of the growth and development of any given society people had always enjoyed to witness many ups and down in the process of their life. Due to this natural phenomenon people had many experience of having high degree of anxiety and stress in their social life. It was mainly because of the apprehension of the possible danger in the maintenance of their distinctive identity. Such type of experience was also occurred in the history of this state. Though it is not required to go into detail about the nature of the growth of the society of this state it is quite evident that right from the last part of the seventeenth and beginning of the eighteen century people of this state had got an unprecedented experience of having a sudden and dramatic change in their whole social and customary life. This situation was created by the emergence of the influence of Hindu religion which was termed by the radical people as the foreign religion. About the nature and character of the tremendous increased of the influence of this religion was already discussed in the preceding chapter. From the evidences it is quite clear that people were forced to accept new religion by the strong initiative of feudal administration. This new phenomenon had produced a serious impact in the social and cultural life of the people and state. Ultimately it gave a great threat to the existence of the distinctive historical identity in the social and cultural life which was in practiced right from the time of the establishment of society. At the same time due to the negative attitude of the religious policy of the leaders of so called foreign religion a serious disturbances was also occurred in the existence of harmonious relationship among the various ethnic group of people in the state. These were the serious issues which were witnessed by the people. But due to the lack of satisfactory social environment people were not able to raise their voice against this undesirable atmosphere. On the other hand such type of uncheck social problems had forced to increase the degree of anxiety and stress among the individuals. At this stage people of this state particularly of radical group began to recall the traditional social behavior and character which were in practiced among the people before the emergence of new religious ideology. They had also started to test the value judgment between distinctive historical tradition and existing social character. The outbreak of such type phenomenon was mainly due to the absence of the expected help and needs from the existing social order. The failure to control or reduce the degree of internal social mechanism ultimately led to the growth of cultural distortion. In the case of this state also people had a strong impression that the practices of new religion had produced a serious distortion in the traditional cultural life. Thus after having a good experience of intolerable stress and anxiety the people of radical group began to express their unhappiness to the existing social and religious system with a more revolutionary character. The tremendous increased in the degree of anxiety and stress among the people of this state was the direct reason for the outbreak of religious revitalization movement. Their only desire was to protect the distinctive historical identity of this state from the distortion policy of the leaders of the new religion.

An ex-revolutionary leader said the adoption of Hinduism was the only reason for the extinction of the separate and distinctive cultural identity of the people of Manipur. Naoria Phullo was the only person who took the leadership of pioneering work. He fully realized the existing the atmosphere of the people in the society. Therefore he adopted a policy of slow pace for a successful mass movement. As a first step he created a situation to reformulate the mindset of the people by giving a new idea of the immediate need to change in the social and religious life of the state. Such type of character is called by many writers as hallucinatory vision which is conceived only to a single individual. From the nature of his philosophy it is quite evident that the only concerned of Phullo was how to check the rapid deteriorating conditions of the society under the existing norms and practices. His only alternative to this question was to bring a new social and religious order so that the people would be able to check such type of undesirable situation. Accordingly with this single agenda he started a serious campaign against the existing social order. No doubt Phullo was a great visionary and dreamer. He reflected all his ideas and vision in his write up. Through this platform he had visualized a new society and culture in the state by changing the religious beliefs and customs. His only weapon was based on a basic proposal to recall the distinctive historical tradition of pre Hinduism period. He vehemently asked to judge the value between existing social life and new emerging concept. Such type of formulation of new mindset is observed as a stage of presenting new mazeway.

From the evidences it can be said that Naoria Phullo was a great visionary and practical dreamer. He fully convinced that to translate his visionary idea and concept could be made possible only when it was transmitted directly to the people. This stage was regarded as the period of communication phase of the movement. It is mentioned that during this period the leader or prophet made an attempt to convince the people by asserting his ideas and philosophy. This is the exact pattern which Phullo was doing. In order to carry the masses he raised certain key issues which were generally considered bad or undesirable and he also made an attempt to give a better alternative.

Thus due to the nature of the work the character of a visionary dreamer began to change as a leader or prophet. This was also happened in the case of Phullo. The persons who strongly believed in his reformulative concept began to treat him as a great preacher. Whatever the case may be through his consistent efforts Phullo was able to establish a good communication with the people and he readily prepared to construct a platform to draw a visionary mental blue-print for an alternative better arrangement. His only desire was to see a drastic change in the social and religious life of the people of this state based on the framework of distinctive historical tradition. Indeed the establishment of *'Apokpa Marup'* as a platform for a better communication among the people was a great significant step towards the materialization of his dream. This was a new phenomenon of the outcome of the transmission of his vision to the people. Such type of period is regarded as the stage of the final preparation for the religious revitalization movement. Through this platform and also in the midst of the very odd social environment he made a tireless campaign for alternative better religious practices in the state. Thus he started the organizational work as an implementing agency for a change in the social and religious life of the people. And from his nature of work people began to treat him as a great charismatic leader.

In the meantime the reformative idea and concept of Naoria Phullo began to cross the existing boundary line i.e. the Cachar District of Assam and many radical people began to welcome his idea and concept. It is a fact that religious revitalization movement always aimed for a revolution. Therefore such type of movement had always encountered strong resistance from those personalities who enjoyed the opportunities from the existing social order. Even though there were a lot of resistance elements in the society,people began to come out openly and started to express their opinion against existing social and religious life in the state. This opportunity and platform enjoyed by the radical people was the contribution of Phullo. Then the radical people began to campaign in favour of primal religious concept and practices with revolutionary tone. The establishment of *'Meetei Marup'* had further intensified the character of the movement and it created a great landmark for the growth of mass uprising against the existing religious and customary practices. Thus the establishment of this organization marked the beginning of the ideological conflict with the *Brahma Sabha* another religious organization of Hindu religion. At the same time it also marked as the beginning of large scale movement for the revitalization of primal religion of this state. This stage is also classified as the phase of adaptation. It is mentioned that at this phase the personalities of radical group of people, with an objective to face any type of resistance from the existing system had used various strategies of adaptation. The strategies may be political maneuver of force and it should be imperative of the organization to maintain it.

At the beginning the leaders of the movement adopted the non-violent and democratic approach as the strategy of the movement. They did not encourage any type of violent method. And through non violent strategy they tried to carry the masses with a nationalistic approach. Their only objective was to bring a drastic change in the existing social and religious environment. Apart from this they also proposed to promote and foster the distinctive historical traditions which were believed in the process of extinction in the hand of foreign religion. However the situation compelled them to accept the confrontations initiated by the personalities of the exiting social and religious system. The continuous debate on the issue of religious philosophy and concept with the leaders of the Hindu religious organization was one of the unique feature of the religious revitalization movement in Manipur. It was a non-violent and democratic method of movement. But the outcome of the debate was so effective in favour of the radical section of the society that it paved a big way for coming of a large number of people towards the side of the revitalization of primal religion. Besides, the successful effort to change the nature of religious festivals from Hindu religious practices to the original form of pre Hinduism period was also a great noteworthy achievement of the movement of the organization. Indeed such type of activities had rendered a great contribution in the process of the maintenance and promotion of the historical identity of the religious and cultural life of the people.

In the meantime the process and activities of the religious movement was further intensified with the emergence of new political and social outlook among younger generation. Such type of highly radical outlook among the educated younger people was observed as the creation of the unexpected and undesirable political atmosphere which was developed just after the integration of this state into Indian Union. They were of the opinion that the present political trend which had disturbed seriously in the natural status of the people of this state was to be continued further without checking in time then the existence of the distinctive identity of Manipuris would be nowhere. With this strong notion in their mind they strongly asserted that all these social and cultural problems faced by the people was the creation of the acceptance of foreign religion. Thus with certain degree of militant attitude and character they began to look forward to the reformative vision and idea of Naoria Phullo as the best alternative for the protection of their identity. This stage is a very important part in the process of the movement. The acceptance of alternative religious ideas and practices was a great signal of the reduction of the deteriorating symptoms of the individuals. The positive response given by the masses to the new code of the visionary reformation is regarded as the stage of cultural transformation. Thus after this new developmental phenomenon among the mindset of the people the nature and character of the movement began to incline in a more militant way. And in the process of the movement the radical people began to confront with the resistance force in many ways. Thus under this circumstances the degree of the character of militancy had increased tremendously in the process of the movement.

During the course of the movement the leaders had adopted various types of strategies and policies which were outside the basic objective of the movement. But these issues were also more or less directly related with the question of the identity of the society. Apart from the reformative idea for the strengthening of primal religion and its practices the people also started to raise the issue for the official recognition of Manipuri language by the central government by inclusion in the provision of the 8th Schedule of the constitution and to replace the Bengali script by the archaic Manipuri script. In a sense such type question was also very important from the issue of the preservation and maintenance of the distinctive identity of the people of this state. From this fact it clearly demonstrates the level of the increasing degree of nationalistic idea particularly among the leadership of the movement. In order to achieve their demand they launched various types of violent movement in the state. Even the some people make an attempt to establish a hypothesis that the burning of library building of the government of Manipur was perhaps due to the negative attitude of the state government in their demand to recognize the archaic Manipuri script officially in place of Bengal script. They also appealed to the people to extend all sorts of possible help for the promotion of archaic Manipuri script. Besides, they had also requested the state government to introduce the said script in every educational institutions of the state. In response to their demand even the state had agreed to introduce it at every school from primary level of class. In a way such type of movement launched within the framework of religious revitalization movement may be regarded as a big stride towards the establishment of a distinctive identity of Manipuri people and its society.

From the above evidences it can be observed that the nature and character of the religious revitalization movement in Manipur was passing through certain environmental situations. As it already has mentioned above about the picture of the mindset of the society at the time of the formulate stage. Therefore the leader or preacher who had strongly advocated for having a better alternative in the social life of the people had started the movement with a single agenda. At this stage Naoria Phullo had pointed out many defective nature and attitude of the Brahmins committed against the people in the society. He simply made an awareness campaign among the people that by using the platform of existing religious principles the Brahmins had exploited their economy and culture. He also reflected his visionary idea in his celebrated writings. There he pointed out many evidences where the Brahmins had exercised their authority by taking the religious position under the existing system. In some contexts he also said that most of the religious rites and rituals conducted by the Brahmins were not in the tune of the religious books of Hindu religion. On the basis of this evidence Naoria Phullo had strongly criticized the nature of the working of the Brahmins who acted outside true principle of their religion. From this fact it is quite clear that Naoria Phullo never criticized the religious principles and philosophy of Hindu religion. And the anti Brahmin stand was the basic motto of the first phase. Then the second phase of the movement was started with the establishment of 'Apokpa Marup' as a platform for giving awareness about the importance of the concept of primal religion of this state. Here the leader began to give the best alternative to protect the people from the hands of Brahmin. Accordingly he started to ask the people to make a comparative value judgment between existing social order and emerging new religious concept and practices of primal religion. At this stage the character of the movement was highly coloured by the anti Hinduism stand. Gradually the scope of the movement began to expand with the spirit of nationalism concept. Interestingly such type of new developmental phenomenon was greatly influenced by the changing political atmosphere of the post-Independence period. Then very soon the people particularly of radical section of the society were again influenced by the militancy character in their approach and concept. In an open letter to the people these radical people said, "Some of our kings have brought many greedy Brahmins who in return brought with them their religious orthodoxy, a false notion of god and goddesses. They have distorted our scientific religion and burned down our library. Caste system was introduced to us, thus division between us started." They strongly asserted that these Brahmins deliberately tried to degenerate the cultural status of the people of both hills and plain to the level of the aboriginal and forced to embrace Indian culture. They also accused the Brahmins for trying to interpret the spirit of nationalism among the indigenous people of the state as tribalism. Thus the undesirable attitude and their nature of work had created a new mindset among the people particularly of radical section of the society to develop a notion of anti-Hinduism stand. Thus with this mindset people began to work against the religious concept and practices of Hinduism.

In the meantime some ultra elements among the radical group again started to raise the question of the establishment of distinctive identity of the state outside the political boundary of Indian Union. With this firm ideological conviction they have started to indulge in the violent method of movement against all norms of the existing constitution. They were of the view that the attempt of the Brahmins to establish a sanskritised cultural society under the Hinduism would give a death blow to the historical cultural identity of the people of Manipur. So only alternative means to protect themselves from this religious and cultural naked invasion was to establish a separate political entity of the state outside the Indian Union. They further argued that if it was so the people would be able to get freedom the threat of cultural and political hegemonistic attitude of the India. Another ex-revolutionary leader said, "The flames of the insurgency broke out mainly because of the anger of the youth at the losing of their traditional, ethnic and cultural identity created by the introduction Vaisnava Hinduism as a state religion with the support of the rules."

From the above evidences it can be suggested that the radical section in the society of this state had carried on the activities of religious revitalization movement with three distinctive dimensional characters. The initial stage of the movement was restricted purely on the concept of anti Brahmin stand. The leader simply pointed out as a part of awareness programme the deteriorating economic and cultural conditions which was created by the Brahmins in the name existing religion. At this phase there was no evidence where the leader criticized the basic philosophy and principle of the Hindu religion. But it is also true that it laid a basic foundation for the growth of the idea of anti-Hinduism. The establishment of 'Meetei Marup' in Manipur as a religious and cultural organization by the radical elements in the society may be taken as the beginning of the second phase of the movement. At this stage the members of the organization began to speak openly against the attitude of the Brahmins for their effort to establish a sanskritised culture in this state. Ultimately they began to assert for the preservation and promotion of traditional culture and religious identity of the indigenous people against the onslaught of so called Hindu imperialism by the radical people. The third stage was started just after having a new political and economic scenario in the state which was developed with the merger of Manipur into the political boundary of Indian Union. The degradation of the political status, domination by the outsiders in the administration of the state, the control of economic life by the traders coming from outside the state, denial of employment to the educated youths etc. were key factors for the growth of such kind of tendency among the people. Therefore deprivation of their democratic political right by the Government of India was treated by the people particularly the educated youths as a deliberate intention of the policy makers of the central government to destroy and distort the distinctive historical identity of the people of this state. So they began to feel that preservation and promotion of their distinctive social and cultural identity could be maintained only when they established a separate political identity of their own outside the political boundary of India. On the basis of this firm conviction even some ultra elements in the society had indulged in the violent type of movement as a means for the achievement of their goal. So on the basis of these observation it can be suggested that the religious revitalization movement started with an anti-Brahmin stand by Naoria Phullo played a major role in the subsequent years for the growth of the idea of self-determination movement in Manipur.

Bibliography

English

A. Lessa and Evon Z.Vogt(ed). *Readers in Comparative Religion, An Anthropological Approach.*

Brian Davis, *Introduction of the Philosophy of Religion.* 1981.

Brian Davis, *Philosophy of Religion, A guide and anthology.* 2000 A.D. Oxford.

Christopher Patridge, *The World's Religion,* 2005.

Collin Hohn J., *Anthropology, Culture. Society and Evolution,* 1975 New Jersey U.S.A.

D.P. Singhal, *Budhism in East Asia,* 1984.

Dictionary of Philosophy, 1984.

Dr. L. Bheigyachandra, *A Critical Study of the Religious Philosophy of the Meities before the advent of Vaisnavism in Manipur,* 1991.

E.B.Taylor, *Dictionary of Anthropology,* 1990.

E.W. Dunn, *The Gazetteer of Manipur,* 1975.

Encyclopedia of Religion and Ethics, Vol No. X.

Eric Hobsbawn and Terrance Ranger (ed) *The Invention of Tradition,* 2002 Cambridge.

Frank Byron Jevons, *The History of Religion.* Reprint, 1985.

Gangmumei Kabui, *History of Manipur.* Vol One. Pre Colonial Period, 1991.

Gangmumei Kamei, *Essays on Primordial Religion,* 2006 New Delhi.

George Beskener (ed.) Hermon KulkeTilman Frasch and Jurgem Lutte *Exploration in the History of South Asia.*

International Encyclopedia of Social Science, Vol.No. 13 .

James Johnstone, *Manipur and Naga Hills.* Reprint, 1990 .

Kailash K.Beri, *History and Culture of South East Asia (Ancient and Medieval),* 1994.

L. Ibungohal Singh, *An Introduction to Manipur,* 1963.

M. Kirti Singh, *Religious Development in Manipur in the 18th and 19th Century,* 1980.

M.N.Srinivas, *Social Change in Modern India,* 1972.

Marx and Engel, *On Religion,* Progrss Publication, 1985.

N. Birchandra, *The Meitei Society, A Study on Traditional life circle ceremonies* 2006.

N. Tombi Singh, *Manipur and the Mainstream,* 1975.

New Encyclopedia of Britanica. Vol No XV.

R. Brown, *Statistical Account of Manipur.* Reprint, 1975.

R.C. Majumdar, *Hindu Colonialism,* 1974.

R.K. Jhallajit Singh, *A History of Manipuri Literature,* 1987.

R.K. Jhallajit Singh, *A Short History of Manipur From 33A.D. to the present time,* 1965.

S. Sasananda, *History of Buddhism in Assam(300B.C.- 1200 A.D.),* 1986.

Sapamcha Sanatomba@ Bheigya (ed.) *The Sanamahism,* 2003.

Saroj Nalini Parret., *Religion of Manipur,* 1980, Calcutta.

Sergei Tokarev, *History of Religion,* Progress Publication, 1989.

T. Tomba, *The Birth and Death*, 1998.

T.C. Hodson, *The Meitheis*. Reprint, 1975.

The Encyclopedia of Philosophy, Vol No. X.

The Last Two Million Years, 1974, London.

W. McCulloch, *Valley of Manipur*. Reprint, 1986.

William P. Scott, *Dictionary of Sociology*, 1999.

Manipuri

Angoba, *Sembi Mukaklei* 2nd Ed., 1980.

Angomba, *Senbi Mukaklei.*

Atombapu Sharma, *Pakhangba,* 1952.

B.Kullachandra Sharma,*Meidingu Garibniwaz/Mayamba,* 2000.

Bheigya Yengkhiba, *Leithak Leikharol,* 1994.

Bijoy Singh, *Meitreibakki Wari.*

Haoba Nonglelkhomba, *Chingu Khongnangthabagi Wangulol,* 1994.

Hijam Ibopishak, *Meitei Bamon Khunthoklon,* 1978.

Imoinu Amasung Manipuri Khunnai, The League of Callow Patiots, 2006.

Irom Amubi Singh, *Awa Ngamba,* 1979.

Irom Amubi Siungh, *Leihou Naophamlon,* 1981.

K.C.Tensuba, *Meitrabak* (*Encyclopedia*), 2008.

Keisam Birchand Singh, *Cheiraoba,* 2000.

Khulem Chandrasekhar, *Inatki Harao Kummei,* 1994.

Khumancha Puyam Iboton, *Kanglei Lik Muthatlakpa,* 1975.

Khumanthem Kaomach Singh, *Manipur Ittibrittee,* 1934.

Konsaba Ibochou, *Ahal Ibungo Takhellamba Bokulgi Sandhonglon Amasung Men Tongba,* 2007.

L. Nandalal Sharma, *Meitrabak*, 1960.

Loitongba Muhindro, *Lainingthou Sanamahi*, 2000.

Longjam Achou Meitei, Angom Ongbi Khuman Tabi Luwang SeidangbiImoinu Ahongbi, 1997.

M.Gourachandra Singh, *Sanamahi Laihui*, 1982.

Mangangmacha Keisham Ibomcha, *Kum Houba*, 1986.

Meetei Lichatki Chatna Pathap, MannabaApunba Marup, 1984.

Meetei Marup Hourakpa Khwai Thoukal Langal Marup, 1945.

Meitei Harao Kummeigi Seminar Paper, Universal Literary Association, 1980.

Moirangthem Chandra Singh, *Panthoibi Khongkul*, 3rd Ed., 1987.

N. Khelchandra Singh, *Ariba Manipuri Longei*, 1978.

N. Khelchandra SinghL.Ibungohal Singh(Ed.), *CheitharolKumbaba*, 1989 (2nd Ed.).

N.Ibochouba Singh A. Chitreshwar Sharma B. Kullachandra Sharma, *Meitei Bamon Hourakpham*, 1995.

N.Khelchandra Singh, *Ariba Manipuri Sahityagi Itihas*, 1992.

Naorem Amuyaima, *Khunung Iratlon*, 1980.

Naoria Phullo, *Ahan Yathang*, 1933.

Naoria Phullo, *Eigi Wareng*, 1985.

Ngariyanbam Kangjia Mangang, *Panthoibi Thilel*, 2006.

Nongthonbamcha Angou Luwang, Ningthou Kangba Lon, 1988.

O.Bhogeshwar Singh, *Ningthourol Lambuba*, 1967.

O.Bhogeshwar Singh, *Sanamahi Laikan* 2nd Ed., 1995.

P. Labango, *Kangleipak Revolution*, 1997.

Pukhrambam Parijat, *Manipur Purabrita*, 1917.

Pukhrambam Parijat, *Manipur Purabrita,* 1985.

Pungdongbam Sundu Moirangaba and Khunaijam Kumar Sakok Lamlen.

Rajkumar Sanaha and Guneshwar, *Manipur Shri Govinda Nirpon* (Meitei Purangi Wa).

Rajkumar Sanahal, *Manipur Itihas,* 1947.

Sairem Nilbir, *Laiyingthou Sanamahi amasung Sanamahi Laing Hinggat Ihou,* 2002.

Sarangthem Bormani, *Meitei Ima Lairembi.*

Sarangthem Bormani, Meitei Ningthourol, Pub., 2000.

Thiokchom Thoukachanpa Pa Meetei, Lalei Lathup Thilel amasung Matamgi Khonglei Puya.

Thokchom Mangoljao, *Manipurda Nongchuplongi Sikha,* 1987.

Thongam Ibotombi, *Hiyangthang Lairembi* (Ireima), 1996.

Thongam Madhop N. Khelchandra, *Khunung Lichat Sajat,* 1970.

Waikhom Romesh, *Kanglei Natki Ariba Masak,* 2006.

Yumnam Tamphajao, *Meetei Lai Haraobagi Wangulon,* 2000.

Index

■■■